# TOLLYMORE

THE STORY OF AN IRISH DEMESNE

# TOLLYMORE

THE STORY OF AN IRISH DEMESNE

*The Earl of Roden*

ULSTER ARCHITECTURAL HERITAGE SOCIETY

*First published in 2005 by*
*The Ulster Architectural Heritage Society*
*66 Donegall Pass, Belfast*

Copyright © Robert Jocelyn, The Earl of Roden

All rights reserved. No part of this publication may be reproduced, stored in a retrieval system or transmitted in any form or by any means, electronic, mechanical, photocopying, scanning, recording or otherwise, without the prior written permission of the copyright holder and publisher of this book.

The Earl of Roden has asserted the moral right to be identified as the author of this work

British Library Cataloguing in Publication Data
A catalogue record of this book is available in the British Library

ISBN: 0 900457 64 3 (hardback)
ISBN: 0 900457 65 1 (softback)

This publication received financial assistance from
The Irish Georgian Society
Edward & Primrose Wilson
Esme Mitchell Trust

Designed by April Sky Design, Newtownards
Printed by W&G Baird Ltd

Photography by James McEvoy
Line drawings by Ebba Kinberg Pate

Front cover:
The south front of Tollymore House in the 1780s. Watercolour by Gerald King based on an engraving by Thomas Milton.

Back cover:
Arms of Viscount Limerick

Title Page:
Inscription on Clanbrassill Bridge

Frontispiece:
The Azalea Walk looking towards the Horn Bridge

# Contents

Preface . . . . . . . . . . . . . . . . . . . . . . . . . . . . . . . . . . . . . . . . . . . . . . vii

Foreword . . . . . . . . . . . . . . . . . . . . . . . . . . . . . . . . . . . . . . . . . . . . ix

Chapter 1 ~ Introduction . . . . . . . . . . . . . . . . . . . . . . . . . . . . . . . 1

Chapter 2 ~ The Early Years . . . . . . . . . . . . . . . . . . . . . . . . . . . 13

Chapter 3 ~ The Limerick Era . . . . . . . . . . . . . . . . . . . . . . . . . 23

Chapter 4 ~ The Clanbrassill Era . . . . . . . . . . . . . . . . . . . . . . . 47

Chapter 5 ~ The Roden Era . . . . . . . . . . . . . . . . . . . . . . . . . . . 93

Chapter 6 ~ The Later Years . . . . . . . . . . . . . . . . . . . . . . . . . 133

Bibliography . . . . . . . . . . . . . . . . . . . . . . . . . . . . . . . . . . . . . 145

Appendices . . . . . . . . . . . . . . . . . . . . . . . . . . . . . . . . . . . . . 154

Site Gazetteer . . . . . . . . . . . . . . . . . . . . . . . . . . . . . . . . . . . 169

*In Memory of*
*Clodagh Countess of Roden*
*who always inspired an interest in Tollymore and its past*

# Preface

Writing this book on Tollymore has been a rewarding odyssey, but it was only when I began in earnest that I realised how vital outside help and direction were to a successful completion. The extensive family archives, now in the Public Record Office in Belfast, were a first port of call yet they only contain snippets of information about the building work at Tollymore, generally as after-thoughts to the more pressing events of the time. What is more, the archive letters are for the most part incoming correspondence. The outgoing letters, which might give a fuller insight into what was happening at Tollymore, were the hardest to track down. To this end I am most grateful to Anthony Malcomson who pointed me in various directions nearly always with fruitful results. He also found time whilst in the middle of his own more substantial and voluminous writing to cast an eye over an early draft. Another person who was unstinting with his help and advice is Harold O'Sullivan in Dundalk whose extensive knowledge of the Magennis family and their times is unequalled.

All books involve a partnership with an editor and publishing house, and I have been most fortunate to have Terence Reeves-Smyth as editor, as his expertise in this field uniquely qualifies him for this project. That he was also able to fit in the editing work with his other commitments, in addition to his peregrinations to far-flung regions of the country and abroad, was truly remarkable.

Many people have been very supportive but I would particularly like to pay tribute to the following for their help; Dr Vernon Armitage of Durham University who supplied me with information on Thomas Wright, Fionntan Gogarty who was quite prepared to dash off home in the middle of a party and return with the answer to a particular problem, Victoria Glendinning who aptly likened writing to block by block construction work, George Hanna whose interest in Tollymore and good humour were always a bonus to research work, Diana Kirkpatrick who provided me with a base and endless hospitality when I needed to visit

Tollymore, Michael Lear for his technical corrections on the arboretum species, John Leyden for the correct Greek translation of the now missing Hermitage plaque, and Isobel McComb who provided the names of those who had worked with her at Tollymore for my grandparents. Also, John and Eileen Harris, James Jocelyn, Johnny Madden, Peter Marlow, Dr Murray Power, Peter Rankin, Noel Ross, Dawson Stelfox, Rod Teck, David Turkington, Irene Whelan and Gordon Wheeler.

When looking for a competent photographer I was most fortunate to be introduced to James McEvoy who lives a few miles from Tollymore. Not only has he provided illustrations from his own private collection but also took the present-day photographs in all weathers and seasons. Ebba Kinberg Pate could not have been more prompt or helpful with the drawings for the book.

I owe a not inconsiderable debt to my wife Ann who checked numerous drafts and was unsparing in her support and advice.

Lastly, I would like to mention the unsung and largely forgotten people without whose efforts and hard-earned rental Tollymore would not have been built when it was - namely the tenant families of the Mournes and Dundalk.

# Foreword

*by*
*the Knight of Glin*

When staying at Seaforde, County Down, in the early 1970s, I remember so well its beautiful demesne with its severe neoclassical house, shimmering lakes, and superb view of the distant Mournes seen through the park framed by rhododendrons and stands of birch trees. Patrick Forde had recently bravely resisted his trustees who advised him to pull down the house and build a convenient new one. Aided and abetted by Mariga Guinness, a number of us 'architectural fanciers', including Paddy Rossmore, set out to explore some of the wonders of south County Down. One of our first expeditions led us to Bryansford and Tollymore Park. Here we found the Gothick gate through which appeared the Clanbrassill Barn with its steeple and a sensational view of wooded hills and valley beyond. The mansion house of the Earls of Roden had been demolished, a fact that I remember made Patrick all the more determined to maintain his! Around the perimeter of the demesne we discovered Lord Limerick's Follies on the Hilltown road, which included pinnacled gate piers, all decorated with granite bap-stones brought up from the Shimna river far below. Paddy Rossmore took photographs of the barn and the Follies, and Edward Malins and I used them in our book on Irish landscape gardening *Lost Demesnes* published some years later in 1976. At the time of our visit we knew little about the extraordinary history of this romantic spot.

In 1955, Tollymore was opened as a Forest Park by the government of Northern Ireland who had bought the estate from the eighth Earl of Roden between 1930 and 1941. An excellent booklet was published in 1972, giving a brief history of the place and chronicling the seminal and important role of the first and second Earls of Clanbrassill as arboriculturists.[1] They introduced many American species, planted the first Norway spruce and founded the great arboretum which contributes to Tollymore's importance today. The second earl had started the idea of reforestation on the remote hills and mountains of Ireland with a commercial coniferous woodland, following the example of the Duke of Atholl at Dunkeld in Scotland.[2] By the 1830s Tollymore was actively producing timber and large quantities were cut to any size and fit for any purpose. A water-driven sawmill was in operation when John O'Donovan, working for the Ordnance Survey, visited Tollymore between 1830 and 1834, and went on to comment: 'His Lordship farms a good deal and has a threshing machine and many other ingenious agricultural instruments'.[3]

The demesne boasts various bridges, the hermitage on the river and the turret follies, already mentioned, one of which acted as a boundary pillar separating Lord Downshire's and Lord Roden's estates. These follies were designed or inspired by Thomas Wright, the amateur architect, antiquarian and astronomer 'the Wizard of Durham' who was a friend of Lord Limerick, later the first Earl of Clanbrassill.

Thomas Wright (1711-1786) is one of the most fascinating figures in the architectural world of the eighteenth century. His connection with Lord Limerick was through Limerick's Dutch wife, Harriet Bentinck, and her relations, who included the second Duke of Portland and the Duke of Kent and the Bishop of Durham. Limerick brought him to Ireland and Wright subsequently published his illustrated pioneering study of Irish antiquities *Louthiana* in 1748. The foremost scholar of Wright, Eileen Harris, is the wife of one of my oldest friends, the English architectural historian, John Harris. She was intrigued to learn more about Wright's Irish travels and described Wright aptly in *Country Life* in 1971: 'There was something flighty and eccentric in his motions and a wildness of fancy followed even his ordinary projects'.[4] His oeuvre also shows the influence of William Kent, particularly in his garden designs.

One can see the fantasy of Wright's work in the picturesque mountainous setting of Tollymore. This sort of romantic setting was becoming all the rage in Ireland in the mid-eighteenth century with the Burkian appreciation of the 'sublime', discovered in such places as the Powerscourt demesne with its great waterfall and the rocky woody fastnesses of the Dargle valley. The Lakes of Killarney were also being revealed and they soon became a mecca for tourists. Lord Limerick and Thomas Wright were pioneers in Ireland of the Gothick Revival. The Bryansford Gate, even though it is dated 1786, the year of Wright's death, is as Michael McCarthy, the distinguished scholar of the Gothic Revival, states: 'so thoroughly Wrightian in feeling that one is convinced of this authorship on stylistic grounds.[5] I also feel that it harks back to the drawings of Richard Bentley for Walpole's Strawberry Hill, particularly a gateway dated 1758'.[6]

Therefore, Tollymore and its garden and buildings are pioneers of the Gothick Revival in Ireland. McCarthy goes on to say: 'none of the buildings at Tollymore bear an exact correspondence with Wright's designs, but they are spiritually his and some allowance must be made for the fertile inventiveness of local masons, or maybe of Limerick himself, in their execution'.[7]

The rocky hermitage by the river may also owe its inspiration to Wright. It was dedicated by Lord Clanbrassill to the Marquis of Monthermer, the eldest son of the Duke of Montagu, whose superb languid portrait, showing him holding a book of music, by Pompeo Batoni still hangs at Boughton in Northamptonshire.

Turning from follies and buildings, Lord Limerick was remarkable for the early importation of plants and seeds from the Americas. He imported magnolias from the Carolinas, shells from Antigua, and cedars of Lebanon, which were consigned in 1752. Lord Limerick, now the Earl of Clanbrassill, retired from public life in 1756 and passionately concentrated on his gardening activities, both in his Dundalk demesne and at Tollymore. In his book, Lord Roden quotes Thomas Jefferson in this context: 'No occupation is so delightful to me as the culture of the earth, and no culture to that of the garden'.

This story of Tollymore continues to the era of the Earls of Roden who descend from the second Earl of Clanbrassill's sister and it evocatively shows the vicissitudes of the family right down to the taking over of the demesne as a Forest Park. It is a book that joins a new array of published studies of Irish demesnes. One must think of Nigel Everett's essays around Bantry Bay and Derreen.[8] Other books, such as Joan Ussher Sharkey's study of St Anne's[9] and Olda FitzGerald's work on Ashford,[10] give a serious recognition to the historical importance of the these properties. A further important recent work is Finola O'Kane's study of amongst other places Castletown and Carton.[11] One must also welcome the establishment of an inventory of historic designed landscapes by the Office of Public Works in Dublin. The National Inventory of Architectural Heritage, also emanating from the OPW, is identifying houses and areas of heritage so that local bodies can attempt to protect them.[12] A study of Irish houses and historic estates has been set up under the leadership of Terence Dooley at the National University of Ireland, Maynooth. All these steps forward are of vital importance as year by year demesnes across the country are being seriously eroded by golf courses and attendant housing developments. More sensitive landscape and design control is vitally needed in Ireland. Much of modern history in this country has tended to overlook the importance of the demesne in Irish culture and craftsmanship. These books can therefore only help to redress this issue.

It is a pleasure to read the story as told by Lord Roden so sensitively about his ancestral property. Would it be that we had this book before our visit to Tollymore from Seaforde so long ago in the early 1970s! One hopes that its publication will influence the ongoing care and attention due this much visited demesne.

1. Department of Agriculture Northern Ireland (Forest Service), (1972). *Tollymore Park Guide.*
2. James Hamilton Earl of Clanbrassill, (1783). *An Account of the Method of Raising and Planting Pinus Sylvestris, that is Scotch Fir or Pine.*
3. *Tollymore Park Guide., op.cit.*, p8.
4. Eileen Harris, (1971). 'The Wizard of Durham: The Architecture of Thomas Wright', *Country Life*, vol. CL, 26th August 1971, p494. See also the entry on Wright by Eileen Harris, (2000). *British Architectural Books and Writers 1556 – 1775*. See also J.A.K. Dean, (1994). *The Gate Lodges of Ulster*, pp 97 –98.
5. Michael McCarthy, (1987). *The Origins of the Gothic Revival.* p46.
6. *ibid.*, p40, plate 36.
7. *ibid.*, p45.
8. Nigel Everett, (1999). *An Irish Arcadia. The Historic Gardens of Bantry House*, Nigel Everett, (2001). *Wild Gardens. The Lost Demesnes of Bantry Bay.* Bantry: Hafod; Nigel Everett, 2001. *A Landlord's Garden, Derreen, Co. Kerry.*
9. Joan Ussher Sharkey, (2002). *St. Anne's: The Study of a Guinness Estate.*
10. Olda FitzGerald, (2001). *Ashford Castle.*
11. Finola O'Kane, (2004). *Landscape Design in Eighteenth Century Ireland*, Cork.
12. Coílín MacLochlainn and Ian Lumley, (2004). 'Vanishing Arcadia', *An Taisce Magazine* (winter), pp16-20.

*CHAPTER 1*

# Introduction

The distinctive Irish demesne, with its designed landscape, woodlands, gardens, architectural embellishments, house and accompanying heritage, is one of Ireland's great contributions to European culture. However, before these demesnes could be created on any scale, the country had to be at peace, and in the 16th and 17th centuries this was far from the case.

It has been said that there is no such disruptive force as a common creed held with a difference.[1] Religious discord coupled with the near absolute power of monarchs in the 17th century meant that there could be no sustained peace throughout Europe. Ireland, for once, was not isolated from the upheavals. After the Williamite army fought its way across Ireland in 1690-91, the last full-scale European war to be contested on Irish soil mercifully came to an end. While the war continued intermittently on the Continent, the overhanging threat of an invasion of the British Isles had been finally lifted. Ireland was sullen and subdued but, deep down, there was a yearning for a halt to hostilities. However imperfect the peace, this peace dividend was to last for over a hundred years. Parliaments, not kings, now made laws. When peace eventually came to the rest of Europe, it very soon brought better trading opportunities, a flowering of artistic talent and new ideas. Handel wrote *The Messiah*, Adam Smith his *Wealth of Nations*, Mozart his concertos. It was the Age of Enlightenment. Gifted amateurs in their hundreds applied themselves to natural history, botany, science, astronomy and architecture. After a thousand years Irish craftsmanship once again excelled. They were exciting times - if you hadn't been marginalised or forced into exile.

Relieved of the need to give priority to their family's protection, owners became more confident and outward-looking. This was evident in the new architectural fashions that appeared in the planning of houses and their demesnes.[2] Property no longer had to be defended. A golden era of building had begun.

Even taking into account the present un-prepossessing ribbon development and new town planning, the creation of Ireland's demesnes was the single most significant man-made change to the Irish landscape. Today, much of the country's mature deciduous woodland lies within their boundaries.[3] Furthermore, this tangible expression of a separate style and culture, which was given added weight by the writings of Jonathan Swift and others, was the first manifestation of a peaceful move towards an equal, self-governing nation that culminated in the Declaration of Independence achieved by Henry Grattan's Irish Parliament of 1782.

The history and development of landed estates and their core demesnes were influenced, not only by local and political events, but also by world affairs. From the Act of Union with England in 1800 onwards, Irish landlords felt under increasing threat from a variety of directions, and it was not just the after-tremors of the recent French Revolution and its excesses. Control from Westminster, agrarian agitation and reform, famine and the collapse of the agricultural economy all had to be addressed at different times. Later, world wars, insurrection and unswept chimneys added to the problems. It is, therefore, hardly surprising that fewer landed estates were amassed during these later years, unless the owner was a successful businessman, or had accumulated his fortune elsewhere.

No understanding of a landed estate in Ireland or Great Britain would be complete without some awareness of the financial structures of the time. In the 17th and 18th centuries, rental derived from land ownership was the primary source of income - with a little patronage thrown in, if it could be acquired.[4] There were few investment opportunities and not many careers outside the church, the army and the law.

The English land system that was introduced into the Irish Lordships during the Elizabethan and Jacobean periods was a progression from the earlier Customary Law that it replaced. But debt was universal. Secured by tenanted holdings, Irish and English landowners incurred inordinate debt for all manner of reasons, entering into mortgage arrangements in the most cavalier fashion, and to an extent quite unthinkable nowadays. At his death in 1798 the second Earl of Clanbrassill had debts of £60,000 (the equivalent of £2,250,000 today).[5] Provided there was a land bank of tenants able to pay rent on demand, such debt was supportable. Even so, numerous landowners fell foul of the Encumbered Estates Court set up in 1849 to try and bring some order to the heavily mortgaged land structure that had been accentuated by the Great Famine. Subsequently, Gladstone's Landlord and Tenant Act of 1870 saw the first tentative start by government to enable tenants to purchase their holdings. With the passage of the

Ashbourne Act of 1885 and the generous buy-out provisions of the Wyndham Act of 1903, most Irish estate lands were sold to their tenants, the transaction being financed by the government.[6] However, too often the money received from the government was used to pay off debts and taxes such as the new inheritance tax, or just frittered away. Without the land bank, the remaining core of the estate, the demesne with its house, gardens and parkland, was soon vulnerable, unless an alternative income was quickly forthcoming.

It has been said that a recurring drain on a family's exchequer were dowagers afflicted with longevity, or worse, an extended family of sons and daughters, all of whom expected handsome capital settlements. Writing to her sister, Lady Louisa Conolly mentioned a possible marriage between one of the family and Lord Jocelyn, later the second Earl of Roden:

> *But if it should, I cannot see the objection but a little want of money which, with so pretty a young man, might be dispensed with. William thinks that his large family must ever make him poor.*[7]

One positive aspect of affairs in the early Irish Lordships was that the successor to the chieftain, whether appointed by force or by agreement, was generally the fittest and fastest past the post. Moreover, the property stayed within the ownership of the clan. It was a system much approved of by, for example, Peter the Great, who ordained that his wife take over the reins of the Russian empire after his death. The English custom of the right of primogeniture required that the eldest son inherit his father's property, irrespective of capability, state of health or suitability for the job. Inevitably, families and their properties suffered as a result.

Given so many political, financial and social problems confronting the large demesnes, more particularly in the 19th and 20th centuries, it is hardly surprising that so few have survived as originally devised. Many a great house has been gutted or pulled down, parkland turned into golf courses or sold for development. These unique landscapes are more easily destroyed than created, yet they are the result of great endeavour and Irish craftsmanship, mostly of a very high standard.

Tollymore, abutting onto the northern flanks of the Mourne Mountains in County Down, was the site of a deer park from around 1710-15 and then flourished as the focus of a great 18th-century demesne before experiencing all the disturbances and trials of the subsequent years. The name Tollymore (*Tulaigh Mhór*) signifies a 'large hill or mound', an apparent reference to twin summits that rise to 256 metres on the southern boundary of the demesne.[8] These two hills, now forested, were recorded by Walter Harris in 1744 as Slieve Neir and

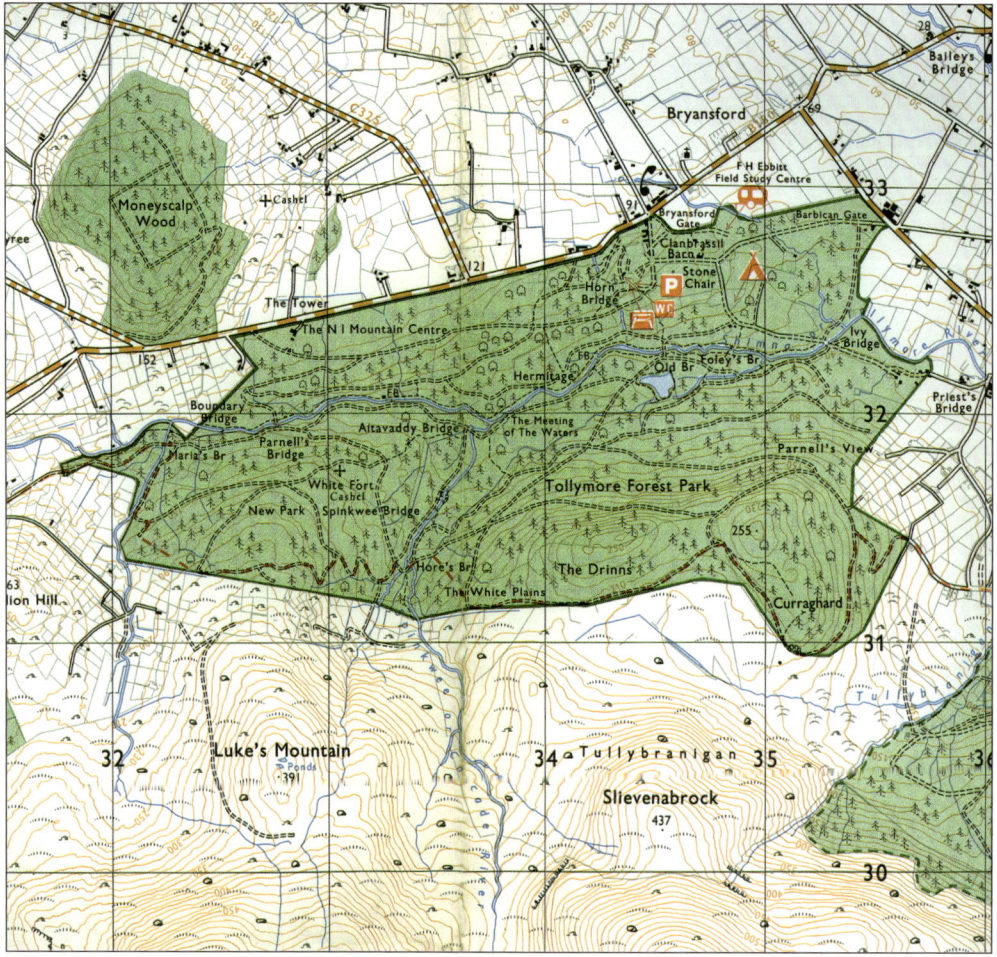

Map showing Tollymore at the foot of the Mournes. *Source: Ordnance Survey Pursuits map 1:25,000, edition 1981. Each grid square is one kilometre. © Crown Copyright*

Slieve Snaran.⁹ Today they are better known as the Drinns and Curraghard, the former meaning 'ridge' and the latter 'marshy upland'; Curraghard is also now known as the Tea House Hill, after a little chalet and stables that once stood near the summit. A dramatic feature of the slopes below is the Tollymore River, or the Shimna River – the 'river of the bulrushes'. This rises in the Deer's Meadow to the south-west and flows some thirteen kilometres down to the sea at Newcastle, passing though the demesne in a roughly west-east direction. Among its tributaries is the Cascade River, sometimes known as the Spinkwee River, which provides a dramatic spectacle of cascades.¹⁰

The boundaries of Tollymore Park townland still largely follow those of the early 18th-century deer park, though some additions were later made on the south-east, east and north-east sides. This account of the demesne has been largely confined to the present townland boundary, which comprises an area of 484 hectares. The home farms, most of Bryansford village and the outlying, tenanted holdings which comprised the rest of the Tollymore Estate have been excluded.

It is a story which begins somewhere in the mists of time when Boirche, the cattle baron of his day, ruled his kingdom from the mountain heights before being laid to rest, so one would like to think, in the King's Grave, a round cairn at the western extremity of the demesne.[11] After a passage of time it continues with the creativity of Viscount Limerick's era, to be followed by the second Earl of Clanbrassill's building and planting. It includes the hundred and forty odd years when it was the main home of the Roden family and finishes when Tollymore became the first, and very popular, amenity park in Northern Ireland.

Tollymore was unusual in Ulster in so far as it was inherited, not expropriated. It came to William Hamilton through his marriage around 1650 to Ellen Magennis whose family owned extensive property in South Down. William and Ellen's grandson, James Hamilton, was created Viscount Limerick in 1719 and subsequently the first Earl of Clanbrassill a few years before he died in 1758. His eldest son, also James, became the second Earl of Clanbrassill, and when he died without an heir, his estates in Ireland and England were passed to his sister, who had married Robert Jocelyn, the first Earl of Roden.

While this book is very much the story of Tollymore rather than a family history, various generations were fundamental to its development, none more so than Viscount Limerick and his son the second Earl of Clanbrassill, who together created most of what can be seen today. Viscount Limerick was only a boy at the start of the 18th century and his son died just before the 1798 Rebellion and subsequent Act of Union. Their lives corresponded almost exactly to the 18th century's remarkable period of peace and prosperity.

By great good fortune Viscount Limerick numbered among his friends one Thomas Wright of Durham. Although he was much younger than Lord Limerick, they shared many ideas and interests. Wright was a man of many parts - an acknowledged astronomer, instrument maker and mathematician, besides being an architect and landscape planner of increasing renown.[12] Their partnership was the catalyst that created Tollymore and the style they both espoused was probably the only one that would have fitted its natural, physical beauty.

Tollymore was never intended to be a 'big house' in the colloquial sense. Viscount Limerick's Irish interests mainly lay in the development of his demesne and gardens in Dundalk. Tollymore, with its old manor and nearby deer park, served primarily as a secondary home and as a sporting retreat.

Many great houses and their demesnes were built, not only to accommodate their owners and families, but also to make a statement that implied wealth and permanence to the world around them. However, Tollymore was the product of aesthetic ideals pursued with a hands-on, creative endeavour. Viscount Limerick, and his son after him, combined successful forestry with the careful enhancement of their demesne. Apart from two small summer-houses, the thatched dining-house and the Hermitage,[13] there were none of the garden follies associated with contemporary English parklands. Such follies as there are at Tollymore are either on, or outside, the boundary walls and generally served specific purposes. Elizabeth Bowen summed up the difference when she compared the demesnes of Cork with their richer neighbours in England:

> *We planted trees effectively but beyond that we had to rely on nature and antiquity. Contours of valleys, reflecting rivers, near mountains have given us something better than the most notable planner could devise. And the monuments of the greater Ireland stand in place of the follies we did not need to build.*[14]

The view northwards from Dundalk towards the southern massif of the Mourne Mountains must have appeared daunting in earlier days, but over and beyond was a picturesque dream in the making. The carriage journey from Dundalk to Tollymore wound up through the Moiry Pass, into Newry and on to Hilltown. It was a long, uphill and far from safe journey. Redmond O'Hanlon, the notorious outlaw, had been tracked down and shot by bounty hunters near Hilltown. Much later, in a journal entry dated 1799, Anne Countess of Roden mentions that:

> *we left Tollymore about nine, and got to Dundalk at four. The mail to the North was robbed at the 45 milestone, just half-an-hour after we passed it.*[15]

Highway robbers remained a problem well into the 19th century. Over the few years prior to 1826, the Newry assizes recorded the capture and trial of seventeen highwaymen. Trundling down the rutted carriageway from Fofany, with jagged mountain peaks set against the right-hand skyline, the first sight of the new fir plantations stretching up from the river must have been a welcoming sight as weary travellers neared their destination.

Tollymore evolved from a deer park designed for hunting, but it was probably the remarkable, natural landscape with the cascading rivers and brooding mountains that aroused Viscount Limerick's interest. The major structural works had already been carried out for him by the Tollymore river and its glacial forebears. In fact, the river plays a major part in the overall scheme of things.

CHAPTER 1

The Shimna river in autumn sunlight

Inscribed Stone near Hore's Bridge

Nowadays it only regains its early passion after a lengthy downpour, having been shorn of much of its headwaters to try and slack Belfast's ever-increasing demand for water. Nonetheless, it can beguile with its quiet moods, or bask in an autumn sunlight. In its heyday it provided power for the numerous flax- and corn-mills in the valley, and worked the sawmill; the remains of mill-races and sluices can still be seen among the undergrowth. Close to the demesne wall the river was harnessed to generate electricity for one of the first houses to have such a facility in Ireland. When there was sufficient water, a run of salmon and seatrout provided excellent sport, and for a while the river held the British Isles' record for a rod-caught seatrout. If all this was not enough, the river also contributed to Tollymore's distinctive architecture, tumbling within its gorges, like a Phidias workshop, the oval, granite bap-stones that ornament most of the buildings in the demesne.[16]

Irish demesnes of the 18th century were constructed on a scale and with a personal commitment rarely found in any other period of the country's history. In most instances, owners were anxious to share and show off their new creations, just as many gardeners do today. Tollymore was always open to the public, but with certain reservations. Guests staying at the village inn were welcome to 'exercise in Tollymore Park on giving their name and applying to the porter at

The Bryansford Gate, circa 1900. The porter standing proudly on the left is dressed in his gate-keeper's uniform with a dark blue top hat. A notice on the gate reads 'Tullymore Park on and after July 1st will only be open to the public to drive or walk on Tuesdays and Fridays from 10am to 6pm. No dogs, bicycles, motor cars or fires allowed in the park'. *Source: The Folk and Transport Museum, Green Collection, 1*

the Bryansford Gate'[17]. In Victorian times Tollymore was open on Tuesdays and Fridays, but visitors were asked to send their jaunting cars back to the village so as not to spoil the grounds for others. On one occasion a prospective group of 300 were asked to choose another day to avoid overcrowding![18] To facilitate the visitors, seats of stone and timber were placed along the popular walks. One visitor in 1834 noted how these seats 'to which you are directed by finger posts' had been placed in various parts of the grounds 'in such places as will afford the best views of the surrounding scenery'.[19]

Much of what was undertaken at Tollymore was well ahead of its time. Viscount Limerick was a pioneer in many fields but, tantalisingly, both he and his son, the second Earl of Clanbrassill, left little documentary evidence of their work. Instead, their legacy is to be found in the 29 kilometres of roadways, the

The Shimna River. Watercolour by Andrew Nicholl circa 1820. *Source: Abbott and Holder*

bridges, arboretum and plantations, and demesne buildings. These are the records they have left for posterity to judge and admire. But there are still unsolved mysteries, like the strange Gothic-arched building abandoned in the woods, or the whereabouts of the original open dining-house. Perhaps Tollymore should be allowed a few secrets, to be puzzled over on a summer evening's walk along the river.

The book is sub-titled *The Story of an Irish Demesne*. It is a story with many facets. How the demesne came into being and how, in turn, it shaped the lives of many of the people who made their home there. It is also the story of how it survived on its own, having been partly abandoned and almost forgotten. And how, even though encroached upon by afforestation and modern facilities, it is still alive and showing off its treasures. Whatever way Tollymore is viewed, I hope that this book will provide an added dimension for all those who know it, that they will have a better understanding of how the demesne was created and why it was done in such a distinctive style. Moreover, I hope the book will prompt others to discover this sylvan idyll first created by the river and then embellished with great care by many generations.

1. Attributed to John Buchan.
2. The word 'demesne' is derived from the old Anglo-French term for that portion of lands which the lord of the manor reserved for his own use and occupation, and which were worked for his own private benefit, see T. Reeves-Smyth (1997a) 'The natural history of demesnes', in J.W. Foster and H.C.G. Chesney (eds.), *Nature in Ireland. A Scientific and Cultural History*, p549.
3. In County Down it has been estimated that over 60% of all broadleaved, mixed and coniferous woodland occurs in demesnes. R. Tomlinson (1997) 'Trees and woodlands of County Down' in L. Proudfoot (ed.), *Down History and Society*, p239.
4. In 1783, 37% of Irish peers held positions granted by the English Parliament. Sadly, the importance of patronage added greatly to absenteeism after the Act of Union, as the opportunities for preferment derived mainly from influence at Westminster.
5. The Roden Papers.
6. See Mark Bence-Jones (1987) *Twilight of the Ascendancy*, especially chapter 5.
7. Undated letter from Lady Louisa Conolly to Emily Duchess of Leinster. Leinster Papers (NLI).
8. Tollymore, formerly known as 'Ballytullymore', was initially divided into two 'half townlands' as early as 1611. Both these 'half townlands' were themselves divided into quarters, namely Carrowlismecaltan and Carrowecharebane (Tollymore Park in Kilcoo Parish) and Carrowlissenefrin and Carrowmurwaghnemucklagh (Tollymore in Maghera Parish). See G. Stockman (ed.) (1993). *Place-names of Northern Ireland, County Down III*, vol. 3, p114.
9. W. Harris (1744). *The Antient and Present State of the County of Down*, p123. Harris ventures that Snaran is in fact Snarvan 'to creep' as the hillside is so steep that it has to 'be climbed in a creeping posture'. It might also be linked to 'snarban' meaning a cataract. It is suggested that Slieve Neir is derived from Sliabh an Aoire 'the mountain of the shepherd'. Tullybranigan is 'Branigan's Hill' and Clonachullion 'the field of the holly'.
10. The Shimna River is depicted on James Kennedy's map of County Down (1755) with the name Hanolock River (PRONI D695/M/2). Other tributaries of this river include the Trassey River ('the fierce one') and Luke's River. The name Spinkwee is probably a hybrid from 'slinnc' meaning crag or cliff.
11. When standing on the King's Grave the winter's sun at midday bisects the broken tors of Slieve Bernagh. For a description of the King's Grave, see Gazetteer site No. 65. The old name for the Mourne Mountains is *Benna Bairche*. There are two versions of how this name arrived. One is the tradition that the mountains were the home of Biorche (Bairche) and that he tended every cow in his kingdom down as far as the River Boyne. The second version relates how Bennan, son of Boirchenn, killed a person called Ibel 'for going in unto his wife Lecon,' only to be killed in his turn in the mountains. Estyn Evans (1951) *Mourne Country. Landscape and Life in South Down*, p103.
12. Thomas Wright (1711-1786). For an outline of his career and principal works, see Howard Colvin (1995) *A Biographical Dictionary of British Architects*, pp1100. Also Harris, Eileen. (1971a), 'The Wizard of Durham: the architecture of Thomas Wright. I'. *Country Life*, vol. CL (No.3872), Aug 26th, pp.492-495; Eileen Harris. (1971b). 'A flair for the grandiose: the

architecture of Thomas Wright. II'. *Country Life*, CL (No.3873), Sept 2nd, pp.546-550; Eileen Harris. (1971c). 'Architect of rococo landscapes: Thomas Wright. III'. *Country Life*, CL (No.3874) Sept 9th, pp.612-615.

13. The Bernard Scalé maps of 1760 and 1777 in the Roden Collection show the two summer-houses and an Old Hermitage (possibly the thatched house), but these buildings no longer exist.
14. Elizabeth Bowen (1942) *Bowen's Court*. George Jocelyn, younger son of the second Earl of Roden, married Thomasina Bowen of Bowen's Court.
15. See Roden, Anne Countess of (1870). *The Diary of Anne, Countess Dowager of Roden from 6th August 1797, to 11th April, 1802*. Anne was the sister of the second Earl of Clanbrassill and had married the first Earl of Roden.
16. The use of bap-stones is an architectural idiosyncrasy of the area. They are so called after the local, oval bread.
17. Instructions for guests staying at the Roden Arms. The Roden Papers.
18. By 1993 the annual number of visitors to Tollymore had exceeded 200,000.
19. *The Dublin Penny Journal*, II (No.2), April 19th (1834), pp348-350. See No. 19 of Gazetteer for one of these stone seats with inscription.

A drawing of the Hermitage, Tollymore, circa 1820. *Source: Glin Collection*

## CHAPTER 2

# The Early Years

*Tollymore. October 1750. An autumn evening drawing in and the raw, east wind turning to drizzle. The carter pulls the sack over his hunched shoulders and inverts his pipe. The load is a heavy one, he thinks to himself. The last one of the day is often like that. Quarry lads, eager to finish their quotas and get to their tea, tend to throw on a few extra blocks. The new cart will take it though. Downhill most of the way now. The drays must know that they will not be back up the mountain tonight and have a good feed of hay waiting for them. The nipper up behind must be feeling the cold, but he'll warm up soon enough. Plenty of work ahead. Nothing to complain about. The bridge is finished. Now there's talk in the quarry about a mansion house going up somewhere across the river. Maybe it was a good idea to have spent the savings on the new wagon after all. There'll be some changes. Nothing but changes. Sure as hell there will be no shortage of granite from where this lot came ...*[1]

MOURNE GRANITE IS YOUNG granite, as any rock climber will explain. But the mountains seen today were once covered with a much older, sedimentary rock that was bit by bit washed and ground away to expose the present peaks.[2] Tollymore is largely composed of that early, Silurian shale that the second Earl of Clanbrassill realised offered a good base and soil for his conifer plantations. Standing on a Mourne summit, with the east wind howling in from the direction of the Isle of Man, it is hard to accept that the sea has such a benign influence on the local climate, but it does. The coastal strip of Ireland has a mean temperature above the inland areas, and this allowed arbutus trees and other specimens more associated with temperate regions to grow well at Tollymore. The great gardens of Ulster are mostly within this coastal belt.

The Mourne district, which includes Tollymore, is rich in local culture and folklore. The hidden valleys, booleying pastures and sea passages nurtured the region's legends and stories.³ Many traditions and ways of life died hard, as even St Patrick discovered. One story relates how he almost met his match when he tried to convert the stubborn chieftain, Donard, who had his home at Maghera, a few kilometres from Tollymore. Patrick, it is said, had to use all his resourcefulness, and only when he had brought back to life a ferocious steer that had been killed, jointed and salted down, did Donard relent, afterwards taking himself off up the mountain that bears his name, where he spent his days in a windswept cell.⁴

*The Annals of Ulster* refer to an earthquake in the Mournes in 600. Ten years later they record that the army of the Ulaid, the overkingdom of south-eastern Ulster, was scattered by a 'terrible thunder'.⁵ The following century an unusual whale was cast ashore that was found to have three gold teeth each weighing 50 ounces, one of which was displayed upon the altarpiece of a local monastery.⁶ If this increased the congregation, its subsequent history has been lost, unless it was taken by the ubiquitous Vikings who were active in the area. They had a settlement in Carlingford Lough, on the other side of the mountains from Tollymore, and their boat-builders left the distinctive double-pointed, clinker-built yawls as their legacy to the Mournes.⁷

*The Annals* use the term *Bairche* for the Mourne district, while the Mourne Mountains were known as *Benna Bairche*, the 'Peaks of Bairche'.⁸ For many centuries the area formed part of the overkingdom of Ulaid, but in 1165 the Dál Fiatach, then rulers of the Ulaid, gifted *Bairche* to the neighbouring Airghilla kingdom in return for their support against the Uí Neill kings, rulers of the area west of the Bann. The King of Airghilla then granted the lands to the Mugdorna, a sept within his own kingdom living at Cremourne in what is now County Monaghan. They subsequently moved eastwards and gave their name to the Mournes.⁹

It was not the first time the Mourne district became a refuge to those on the move. However, the marginal land provided sparse nourishment for animals, and the inhabitants had to be continually on their guard from cattle thieves and raiders. In Tollymore, a little off the road between Hore's Bridge and Parnell's Bridge, is a large circular enclosure, or cashel, known as the 'White Fort'. It measures 44m x 54m in diameter with walls over 3m thick. Even today the wall is 2m high, so it must have been over twice that height when occupied. The enclosure would have been in use during early Christian times, perhaps until 1000 AD, or even longer.

The Mugdorna were not long settled in the Mournes when the Normans

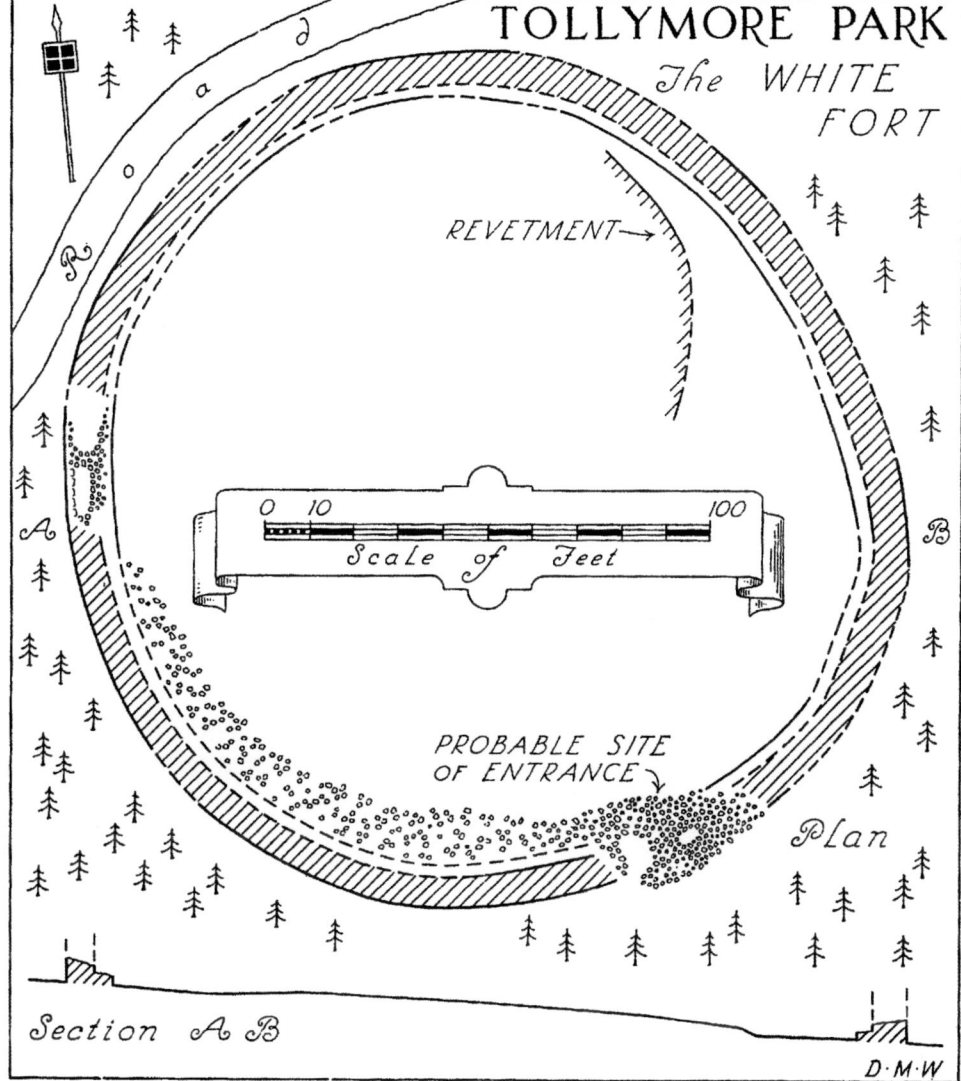

The circular cashel at Tollymore, known as the 'White Fort'. Source: Plan by Dudley Waterman in the *Archaeological Survey of County Down*, 1966

stormed into Ulster in 1177 under John de Courcy. The mountain areas were probably not greatly effected by the new arrivals, but the creation of the Earldom of Ulster did provide an opportunity for the Magennises to establish a power base in Iveagh and become the leading Irish clan in south-east Ulster. By the 15th century they had extended their control over much of south Down, but they were split into numerous extended families, often vying with one another for overall control.[9]

In 1541 a policy of surrender and regrant of property was introduced which involved the Irish chieftains being granted formal freeholds on surrendering their lands to the English crown. It may have simplified the *de facto* state of affairs, but the devil was in the detail. Among other conditions, the regrant was subject to the forfeiture of the property in the event of an owner's involvement, known or suspected, in insurrection or rebellion.[10]

One such deed, drawn up in Latin on the 22nd February 1611, included 'Ballytullymore' (Tollymore) in a grant of seven and a half townlands to Brian McHugh McAghorley Magennis.[11] These lands, located in the parishes of Kilcoo and Maghera, had been in the Magennis family for generations.[12] Brian McHugh's grandson Bernard, a Protestant, succeeded to the property in 1628, but he died without issue in the 1660s, so the property passed to his aunt Ellen Magennis, Brian McHugh's only daughter. As Ellen was married to William Hamilton, Lord Limerick's grandfather, the property passed into Hamilton family hands.

The seven and a half townlands, which included Tollymore, was the only Magennis property not to be confiscated after the 1641 uprising. In a transfer deed dated 1674, Tollymore is described as having 300 plantation acres 'of wood and underwood, 200 acres of furze and heath, and 200 acres of moors' - on paper hardly the most desirable of properties.[13] The present demesne, which corresponds with the townland boundary of Tollymore Park, covers some 484 hectares and is eight kilometres in circumference. This forms the western portion of the original townland of Ballytullymore, while the eastern part is occupied by the present townland of Tollymore, which has an area of 218 hectares.[14]

William Hamilton came from Erinagh in Lecale, County Down.[15] He was descended from one of the many Scottish branches of the family that settled in Ireland during the Elizabethan and Jacobean period and was closely related to James Hamilton, Viscount Claneboye, whose son and grandson became the first and second Earls of Clanbrassill of the first creation.[16] William Hamilton's son James, Lord Limerick's father, acquired the Tollymore property in 1674, though prior to his death in the 1660s Bernard Maginnis had sought to leave the lands to a male member of his own family.[17] The following year James was granted the right to hold fairs at Tollymore Manor.[18]

Absorbed with trying to claim, reclaim or hold onto their properties, Irish landowners were, for the most part, probably unaware of the significance of what was happening in France towards the end of the 17th century, where trouble was in the making. Louis XIV was determined to secure France's borders and invaded the Low Countries in order to achieve this. In dire straits, the Dutch, under the command of William of Orange, flooded their country, thereby thwarting Louis's invasion plans. From that point on, William's energies were devoted to restricting Louis XIV's ambitions. When James II fled England and William

Half-length portrait of James Hamilton, dated 1686, artist unknown

was installed as king, Louis made common cause with James, giving him aid and encouragement to recover the English throne, the idea being to invade via Ireland. Shortly after his arrival in Dublin in March 1689, James summoned a parliament known as the Patriot Parliament. One of its first enactments was the reversal of the land grants.

Tollymore, among many other estate lands, was declared forfeit, no doubt because in February 1689 James Hamilton had been commissioned as a Colonel to raise a regiment of foot in support of William of Orange. Subsequently, he became Governor of County Down and supplied the Williamite army with provisions. This army included troops of the Duke of Schomberg, William's able and experienced general, who arrived in County Down in August 1689 with ten thousand men. King James, backed by France, faced William who had the unlikely support of the Holy Roman Empire and Spain. The war by-passed County Down and culminated in the defeat of James's forces at the battles of the Boyne and Aughrim in 1690.

During the 1690s James Hamilton of Tollymore had an active and successful political career, sitting as MP for Downpatrick (1692-3) and County Down (1695-9). He was also appointed a commissioner to examine forfeited lands in 1699, most of which were naturally contested by one or more claimants. Undoubtedly he benefited from his marriage in 1689 to Anne Mordaunt, for this helped his social standing, since both her parents were from distinguished English families.[19] Anne Mordaunt's father survived the turmoil of the 17th century by the narrowest of margins. Locked up in the Tower of London by Cromwell, he was brought to trial for high treason accused of being involved in the planned restoration of the monarchy. Thanks in no small measure to Anne's mother, a celebrated beauty, he was acquitted when one of the presiding judges who was likely to declare against Viscount Mordaunt excused himself at the moment of passing sentence. His co-conspirators were not so lucky and were condemned to 'cruel and ignominious deaths'. Mordaunt was remanded to the Tower of London a second time. Another trial was ordered but subsequently dropped on Cromwell's orders. On the king's return he was given high office in the new administration, only to face impeachment in 1666, the year Anne was born. Before the trial could take place, Parliament was prorogued and he was set free.[20] The 17th century was no place for the faint-hearted in either England or Ireland!

Sadly, Anne was widowed while still in her thirties, for James Hamilton died in 1701. Thereafter, she devoted her life to improving the family fortunes and bringing up her three daughters and her son, James Hamilton, later in 1719 created Viscount Limerick.

The family history, written in 1835, describes Anne as a 'clever, sensible, managing person, which is evidently shown by her letters, most addressed to her husband during his long absences in England'.[21] The first tranche of land,

CHAPTER 2

The hermitage with the Shimna River below. Watercolour by William Nicholl, circa 1830.
*Source: Abbott and Holder*

that was later to become the Dundalk Estate, was bought by her husband in 1692. The property, like many others in Ireland at that time, was in a very 'ruinous' condition and had 'suffered much in the late wars'. After her husband's death, Anne increased the estate to over 2,800 hectares through the purchase of adjoining properties, thereby giving the family ownership of the greater part of Dundalk.

In the town Anne founded a school for the education 'of twenty boys and twenty girls'. But it was the education and upbringing of her own children, and her eldest son in particular, that became her main responsibility. Without a doubt, Limerick's distinguished career owed much to her guidance and encouragement. He was sent to Oxford University, from which he graduated in 1712 and for a time studied law. When he reached his majority in 1715, he was returned as MP for Dundalk, holding the seat until 1719. Thereafter he sat in the Irish House of Lords.

At this juncture, the Hamiltons' home was the Manor House, which is located over one kilometre east of the Barbican gate in the adjacent townland of Tollymore in Maghera Parish. It may have been the family home from around

1675 and, if so, was probably also the site of the earlier Magennis residence. The present building, which has an early 18th-century appearance, is a substantial gabled house with a symmetrical two storey five bay front. It faces east with its gabled end on the south side of the Middle Tollymore Road.[22] The grounds, which appear to have been laid out in geometric fashion, incorporate two walled gardens, one of which is dated 1726.[23] On the south-west side, on axis with the house front, are the traces of what appears to have been a long ornamental canal - a feature typical of many early garden layouts. In 1714, when Lord Molesworth was creating his grand formal gardens at Breckdenstown in County Dublin, he mentioned a canal here in a letter to his wife, saying that:

> Mr Stew[art] has been in the north at Mrs Hamilton's of Tullamore where he saw a most noble canal 300 or 400 yards long made by her gardener, an Englishman and a very understanding man...whenever he heard it (our canal) was to be begun, he would come into this country to assist us. He says that there are many very understanding workmen of this country to be had, so that you need not be at the expense of bringing anyone out of England for it, at least before you hear and see these here.[24]

Once again it is possible to discern Anne Hamilton's influence, perhaps more particularly in the construction of the Dundalk gardens. Although Tollymore Park was over one kilometre from the Manor House, it was still only a hilly area of rough pasturage where sheep and goats were grazed on the lower slopes. The local goats' whey, or milk, was a nutritious health drink that at the time was 'prescribed by Physicians in scorbutic and nephritic ailments, as well as disorders of the lungs'.[25] People came especially to Tollymore and the surrounding districts to take whey, particularly in the early summer months, when the goats fed on the wild flowers.[26] But as Dundalk was developed, and Lord Limerick extended his education and interests, this area of 'wood, underwood, furze and heath' would change completely.

1. Composed by the author.
2. The ten peaks in the centre of the Mournes have an average height of 716 metres; the highest is Slieve Donard at 852 metres. Mourne granite was formed in the Tertiary era, 2 to 65 million years ago. The glaciation of the valley can be seen from time to time in the distinctive moraines running parallel to the river.
3. Estyn Evans (1951) *Mourne Country Landscape and Life in South Down*, especially chapter 14.
4. G. Stockman (ed.) (1993) *Place-names of Northern Ireland, County Down III*, vol. 3, p155-7. Donard is believed by some to have been a real historical character who lived in the late 5th and early 6th centuries.
5. *Annals of Ulster from Earliest Times to the Year 1541.* Reprint 1998. Vol. 1, p79 & p87.
6. In the year 739 according to *The Four Masters. Annals of the Kingdom of Ireland from the Earliest Times to the Year 1616.* Third Edition (1887). Vol. 1, p341. In the Norman period Giraldus Cambrensis also mentioned a whale being beached off Carlingford.
7. Evans (1951) *op. cit.*, p160; p182.
8. The old kingdom of *Bairche* is believed to have occupied roughly the same area as the present barony of Mourne. The spelling follows that used in *The Annals*; other spelling variations include *Bairrche* and *Boirche*.
9. T.E. McNeill (1997) 'County Down in the later middle ages' in Proudfoot (ed.), *Down History and Society*, pp.104-106; see also *Annals of Ulster, op cit.*, vol. 2, p151; *Four Masters, op.cit.*, vol. 2, p1155.
10. Harold O'Sullivan (1997) 'The Magennis lordship of Iveagh in the early modern period, 1534 to 1691' in L. Proudfoot (ed.) *Down History and Society*, pp159-202.
11. The Magennises, like other clans, had difficulty at first with the switch over to the English system of land tenure. Well into the 16th century, the common currency was cattle, but then marriage settlements, education, and legal costs following forfeiture all required ready money. This usually meant indebtedness, which many of the old order were unable to repay. A number of Magennises ended up as tenants of their own property. Influence in the right places was all important, but by the time their land had been taken, it was often too late to recover it.
12. *Irish Patent Rolls of James I.* Facsimile of the Irish Record Commission's Calender (1966), p193. Pat. 8 James I. Part 5, 22$^{nd}$ February 1611. The townland is therein called Ballytullymore 'all parcel of Muntereddy with common pasture through the whole mountain or waste of Beannyborfry in Iveagh'. Brian McHugh McAghorley Magennis is first mentioned as owner of Ballytullymore in a schedule of freeholders dated January 1608, *Patent Rolls, op.cit.*,, p.395. Pat. 16, XV.
13. Transfer of lands to James Hamilton and his father William, dated 25$^{th}$ April, 1674. A Plantation or Irish acre is 70,560 sq. ft, much larger than an English (statute or standard) acre of 43,560 sq. ft. Thus 300 Irish acres is equivalent to 485 statute acres (196 hectares) and 700 Irish acres is 1134 statute acres (459 hectares).
14. 218 hectares (538 acres) and 484 hectares (1195 acres). The term 'Tollymore Park' was first used in a grant to Phelim Magennis, son of Brian Magennis, dated December 1620. *Patent Rolls, op. cit.*, Pat 18, XXI-51, p481.

15. In the Parish of Bright, see W. Montgomery (1869) *The Montgomery Manuscripts 1608-1706*, p372.
16. According to Emily Reilly, William of Erinagh was a nephew of William, first Viscount Claneboye, see E. Reilly (1835) *Historical Anecdotes of the Families at Tollymore Park*. Both Clandeboye (Claneboye) and Clanbrassill were originally Magennis lands bordering Lough Neagh. The Clanbrassill title was always spelt with two 'l's.
17. Deed dated 13th December 1674. Tollymore passes from Bernard Magennis to James Hamilton, but he is 'persuaded by others' to leave same to Con Magennis, who then renounces all claim for 'threescore pounds'.
18. E.M. Johnston-Liik (2002) *The History of the Irish Parliament 1692-1800: Commons, Constituencies and Statutes*, vol. 3, p339-340.
19. Anne's mother's family were Careys who were closely associated with several English monarchs. The line goes back to Mary, sister of Anne Boleyn, wife of Henry VIII. Anne's brother became the Earl of Peterborough and Monmouth.
20. Reilly (1835) *op.cit*.
21. Reilly (1835) *op.cit.*, also correspondence from James Hamilton of Tollymore to his wife Anne Mordaunt (1696-1698) in the Roden Papers.
22. Monuments and Buildings Record (BH:EHS); Listed Buildings Database, HB18/13/060. The house was completely renovated around 1950 and incorporates a number of 19th- and 20th-century alterations and extensions. In the Victorian and Edwardian era it belonged to the de Spalier family.
23. The date stone of 1726, formerly placed in an arched gateway in the walled garden to the north of the house, is presently missing. It is possible that this is the datestone presently in the garden in Tollymore Demesne inscribed '1726'.
24. From the Molesworth papers as quoted in E. Malins and The Knight of Glin (1976) *Lost Demesnes: Irish Landscape Gardening 1660-1845*, p15. The letter was dated 12 June, 1714.
25. W. Harris (1744) *The Antient and Present State of the County of Down*, pp.178-9.
26. Goats' whey was, however, looked upon with scepticism by some. Writing to Anne Hamilton, Emily Duchess of Leinster admonished her for drinking whey. 'How dare you write when you drink the goats' whey. I'll complain to Lady Limerick of you'. (24.8.1749). Roden Papers.

*CHAPTER 3*

# The Limerick Era

*May 30th 1716. I left Paris on my way to Fontainebleau. I passed several fine estates lying upon the Seine, all of them have avenues that reach to the road and most of them have handsome parks. There is an avenue of five or six leagues that leads to the palace.*

So reads the first Grand Tour diary entry of James Hamilton, soon to become Viscount Limerick. The fashion he observed for geometric layouts incorporating straight avenues would have been familiar to him in Ireland, though not on this scale. Indeed, the long canal and formal gardens at his mother's house reflected this style. Lord Limerick himself was probably responsible for building a straight avenue that is graphically depicted on Scalé's 1760 map of Tollymore. This once extended through the park for about one and a half kilometres, from the northern entrance to the river, across the Old Bridge, and up a clearly defined gap between the woodlands. There were also straight rides and vistas cut through the park woods to facilitate hunting, not dissimilar to features that Lord Limerick would have seen in the chateaux parks along the Seine and the Loire valleys.

At the turn of the new century both James II and William III died within six months of each other. Queen Anne ascended the throne and her short but remarkable reign began. The Duke of Marlborough continued the war on the Continent with greater success than William III had ever enjoyed, while the capable parliamentarian, the first Lord Godolphin, looked after matters at home. The power of the French with all its attendant threats was finally broken and the great 'Sun King', Louis XIV, died the year before Limerick set out on the road to Fontainebleau.

Apart from the Duke of Marlborough's foot-weary army and those biding their time in exile, much of the Continent had been largely closed to travellers for a generation or more. With the coming of peace both at home and on the

Half-length portrait of Lord Limerick in smoking hat and embroidered coat by Francesco Trevisani, Rome, circa 1720

Continent it was now easier to travel and absorb knowledge at first hand in the true classical tradition. This classical notion of scholarship emphasized the education of the senses on site after a lengthy tutored preparation, or often with a tutor as a companion, rather than cramming the mind with facts in the confines of a study. Thirty kilometres of sea and some dusty roads were all that lay between the relative isolation of the British Isles and the splendours of France and beyond. The Grand Tour became an integral part of a young nobleman's upbringing and it is likely that Anne Hamilton encouraged her only son in this direction. His diaries show that he travelled in France in 1716. He was in Brussels, France and Spain in 1723, where his numerous hand-written passports show him travelling as 'El Conde de Limbreck'. He also travelled in Italy.[1] There is a fine portrait of Limerick in his embroidered smoking jacket, painted by Francesco Trevisani, but

Old Bridge with flanking Suspension Bridges, one each side. *Source: Postcard, circa 1910*

this is undated. Trevisani worked in Rome and was much sought after by visitors to the Eternal City in the 1720s. The parks, palaces, classical landscapes and way of life were all carefully recorded by the young tourist and would influence his ideas and plans in the years ahead.

The 1720s were one of the busiest periods in Limerick's life. Besides travelling on the Continent, he organised the rebuilding of Dundalk, including the preparation of plans for a harbour and new industries in the town.[2] He also began upgrading the deer park at Tollymore, notably adding a stone bridge in 1726 on the long avenue in line with the northern entrance gate.

At its full extent the deer park covered 439 hectares and was divided into two separate areas by a wall carried through the middle of it. The creation of this park, with its many kilometres of walling, must have involved a very considerable financial outlay. However, there are no surviving records for the construction of the earlier eastern portion of the deer park, covering 297 hectares, but this was probably built around 1710-15.[3] The 'New Deer Park', some 140 hectares in extent, was added in 1740, as is indicated in payments made to stone masons during that year for 'work on the deerpark wall'.[4] There is also a payment that year to a tenant for 'loss of ground taken from him by the "New Deerpark"'.⁵ The two parks were noted by Walter Harris during his visit in the early 1740s. He also remarked upon its 'excellent venison' and the fine woods, which he noted were 'cut into ridings and vistoes'.⁶ It seems likely that these woods, whose 'ridings and vistoes' are shown on Scalé's 1760 map, were for the most part well established at the time; no doubt they formed part of the 300 Plantation or Irish acres of woodlands that were recorded in the townland during 1674.

Limerick's alterations to the park during the 1720s were probably mainly directed at improving its use for hunting and recreation. The stone bridge, which bears the inscription 'IH 1726', allowed easy access to the mountain slopes south of the river. It was mentioned by both Harris in 1744 and again by Pococke in 1752, the latter noting the 'handsome bridge', where the rocky cliffs 'on each side may be twenty feet deep' and were so 'covered with trees you can hardly see the water at the bottom in some places'.⁷ There is another plaque set into the bridge showing that it was repaired in 1822; this probably included the indented parapet which is later than the original structure. In the 19th century two suspension bridges were added on either side and supported by iron fixtures that can still be seen below the stone arch. Apart from the fashion at the time to construct suspension bridges (there were four over the river at Tollymore) the reason for their existence is not clear.⁸

No sooner had Limerick completed the bridge than he ordered his first 'parcel' of trees from Holland. Some 11,000 trees were dispatched from Rotterdam in November 1728 along with a consignment of wine.⁹ These trees were probably intended for the deer park and may have formed part of the plantations along its northern side that are depicted on Scalé's 1760 map. But trees and wine were not Limerick's only interest in Holland, because in the same year, at The Hague, he married Harriet Bentinck. The Bentincks were a long-established Dutch family and Harriet's brother became the first Duke of Portland.¹⁰ The connections arising from his marriage were to have a considerable bearing on Limerick's activities, especially as far as Tollymore was concerned.

Their son, James, was born in 1730. That same year an eighteen-year-old instrument-maker and mathematician, named Thomas Wright, thought of becoming a sailor and embarked on a merchantman also bound for Holland. He recorded that he was 'extremely delighted with ye Horizon and Sea' but the crossing disagreed with him and he was 'very near being cast away (by Canting of ye Ballast) in a very great storm'. On his safe arrival in Amsterdam he 'took great Notice of ye Stat House, the Globe and Hemisphere and Geographical

'A Survey of Tollymore Park' by Bernard Scalé, dated 1760

Pavement figure'. Wright was born in Durham and after a varied schooling was at one time apprenticed to a clock-maker.[11] His journal relates that as a boy he was 'much in love with Mathamaticks' and 'very much given to ye Amusement of Drawing, Planning of Maps and Buildings'. By the age of twenty he had set up his own school of navigation and mathematics to try and make a living for himself. Between 1732 and 1733 he redesigned an estate, published almanacs and made calculations of the eclipses of the moon and the sun.[12] It was not surprising that Wright came to the attention of the Earl of Scarbrough, who lived nearby at Lumley Castle, and it was he who provided the openings that Wright so badly needed. Not only did he arrange for Wright's marine theories to be brought to the attention of the Admiralty, but he introduced him to the Prince of Wales and numerous men of position who were to support him throughout his career.

One of Wright's important patrons was Henry de Grey, Duke of Kent, who had married Lady Limerick's sister, Sophia, the same year as Harriet was married in Holland.[13] Another patron was the second Duke of Portland, Harriet's nephew.

Engraving of Thomas Wright of Durham by Paul Fourdrinier from a painting by George Allen of Darlington. *Source: Opposite title page of Clavis Coelestis. London, 1742*

The links continued well into Wright's retirement when her niece, Sophia, married John Egerton who became the Bishop of Durham.[14] Although he had suffered from an early speech impediment, Wright must have had an engaging manner, as the Duke and Duchess of Kent were particularly fond of and generous towards him. He tutored their children, was entertained by them at their various homes and designed alterations for their house in Old Windsor. Wright is depicted as being a congenial and good-humoured man. 'His temper was gentle and affable and his mind was generous'.[15]

With so many family connections it was inevitable that Thomas Wright would soon meet up with Limerick. The coming together of two original and enquiring minds created a partnership which endured for years to come and was continued by Limerick's son, whom Wright tutored and introduced to architectural craftsmanship.

In his diary Limerick recorded that at Fontainebleau there was a small park 'or rather a large garden' within the forest that was walled in. He observed that it was:

> *beautified with very fine hedges, and a noble canal that reaches almost the whole length of it. There is a place they call the meadow in it that is full of fountains; the King used to bring all his court to a fountain in the park where he ordered little fish to be put to see them catch'd and eat by a crane. The House has nothing to recommend it but its bigness. The King's apartments and those of Madame de Berry are handsome. As for the rest of the House it is very indifferent.*

This was Limerick's first recorded encounter with the rigid, classical discipline of French architecture. It was a discipline which had influenced much of France's great artistic contributions to European culture up to that time. But a reaction to this authoritarian grandeur slowly emerged and, like so many revolutions in fashion, the seeds of change had been sown in the preceding era.

During the height of Classicism in France two celebrated artists were pursuing their careers. One was Nicolas Poussin and the other Claude Lorrain. Initially, Poussin was involved with State commissions, work on the Louvre and endless altarpieces, but when he broke away on his own he concentrated on landscape painting, achieving an impression of calmness and simplicity. Poussin left Paris and went to work in Rome where his friend, Claude Lorrain, had been living since he was a boy. In his paintings, Lorrain expressed a deep feeling for the beauty of the Italian countryside using landscape to evoke a sense of serenity in spacious, classical panoramas. Lorrain subsequently became an inspiration to 18th-century landscape designers in what became known as the Picturesque Movement.[16] His work was much sought after by visitors to Rome, and in Limerick's collection of pictures that later hung at Tollymore, there were two landscapes by Claude Lorrain.

The influence of landscape painting, impressions from the Grand Tour and the output of philosophers and poets had, initially, a greater impact on 18th-century landscape planning that that of architects and garden designers. Joseph Addison, the editor of *The Spectator*, took up the theme in his essays. In 1712 he advocated the irregular and 'beautiful Wilderness of Nature, without affecting the nicer Elegancies of Art'. His contemporary, Alexander Pope, explored the question of the Genius of Place imploring planners not to ignore the topographical features of landscape:[17]

> To build, to plant whatever you intend,
> 
> To rear the Column, or the Arch to bend,
> 
> To swell the Terras, or to sink the Grot;
> 
> In all, let Nature never be forgot.

> But treat the Goddess like a modest fair,
> Nor over-dress, nor leave her wholly bare;
> Let not each beauty ev'ry where be spy'd,
> Where half the skill is decently to hide.
> He gains all points, who pleasingly confounds,
> Surprizes, varies, and conceals the Bounds.
> Consult the Genius of the Place in all;
> That tells the waters or to rise, or fall,
> Or helps th'ambitious Hill the heav'ns to scale,
> Or scoops in circling theatres the Vale;
> Calls in the Country, catches op'ning glades,
> Joins willing woods, and varies shades from shades;
> Now breaks, or now directs, th'intending Lines,
> Paints as you plant, and as you work, designs.
> Still follow Sense, of ev'ry Art the Soul,
> Parts answ'ring parts shall slide into a whole,
> Spontaneous beauties all around advance,
> Start ev'n from Difficulty, strike from Chance;
> Nature shall join you; Time shall make it grow
> A Work to wonder at - perhaps a STOW.

Pope acquired a garden of some two hectares at Twickenham in 1719 and proceeded to put his theories into practice. Dean Swift stayed there and maintained a long, literary correspondence with his friend thereafter. Swift carried the torch to Ireland and created his own garden close to St Patrick's Cathedral.[18] Among Swift's circle of friends were the Delanys who spent their time between Mount Panther, ten kilometres from Tollymore, and Delville, their home at Glasnevin outside Dublin. Dr Patrick Delany was a Fellow of Trinity and later Dean of Down. The Delanys were influential figures in Irish landscape design and Mrs Delany also happened to be a cousin of Grace Foley, Limerick's future daughter-in-law.

In 1732 Limerick brought an unusual visitor to Tollymore - the *bon viveur* Edward Walpole. He was the second son of Sir Robert Walpole, the first English Prime Minister. Sir Robert's path would cross with Limerick's in unusual circumstances at a later date. Before he left Tollymore, Edward wrote to thank his host for his hospitality:

*Monday, August 28th 1732.*

*My Lord,*

*I cannot leave this agreeable place, which I shall do tomorrow, without paying my respects to your Lordship in this manner and acknowledging the obligations I have to you, for the great pleasure this part of your territories has afforded me. And I believe indeed that the rest of your Lordship's good intentions to me, in regard to my health, had been as fully answered if it had not been too late in the season for the goat's whey to take its proper effect. But certainly it requires more time than I have had, hotter weather and the earlier part of the summer for it to purify the blood in any great degree. As it is, it has done me some good and I think refreshed my blood. But this is troubling your Lordship with too many particulars concerning myself especially when I have so many better subjects to entertain you with. A description of the beauties of your Park would really deserve a large share in my letter. And I should certainly be tempted to give you a poetical sketch of the whole place if I had not stuffed myself so much with your venison and mutton that I find my genius vastly blunted and very unequal at present to such an attempt. So that if I don't do justice to the Park, which I am mightily taken with, it's its own fault. I imagine by this time you'll be glad to burn this letter, therefore I will take no more of your time than just to make my compliments to Lady Limerick and tell her that they have made me learn Pickett here, that I am entered at Whist, and that I am dreadfully afraid that in another month I shall be able to lose my money at Quadrille. Tho' I hope to see her allways too well to have any such occasion for a card table as she had when I had the honour to be let in constantly among the number of your friends, which favour I shall allways be very sensible of and allways proud of subscribing myself.*

*My Lord,*
*Your Lordship's*
*Most obedient humble servant*
*Edw'd Walpole.*[19]

Edward's younger brother, Horace Walpole, was born in 1717. Unlike his robust father, Horace was a small, frail man with an acerbic wit, who preferred a literary life to politics. After travelling extensively on the Continent he settled at Strawberry Hill, not far from Pope's garden near Twickenham and, in the mid-18th century, became a major influence on the later, Gothic-revival movement.[20]

The original Gothic architecture, as seen in the magnificent cathedrals and palaces of the Middle Ages, had not entirely died out. Country craftsmen still constructed church roofs and barns in the original manner. So, when owners wanted to commission something less formal for their properties, the flexible and individualistic Gothic style of architecture was an available alternative. It had always been around and was there ready to be re-developed. Amongst the cognoscenti there now was an eagerness for something quite different, both in an historical and geographical context, after the long period of Classicism. The pointed archways and castellated turrets of Gothic architecture also engendered a nostalgia for the past and an irreverent freedom which could not be found in the rather out-worn and comparatively restricted Classical designs.

This alternative style was first applied to parkland and garden buildings that could be allowed a certain indulgence. In effect they became testing grounds for a more fully-fledged architectural movement that became popular from the 1730s onwards. It was taken up and given added impetus by gentleman architects, such as Limerick and his son after him, who developed their own amateur architectural skills. In addition, there were numerous illustrated publications on the market that helped promote these new designs which could be browsed over at leisure. They, in turn, were adapted and interpreted to suit the Irish landscape, and materials that were at hand. In a theme echoed by Elizabeth Bowen several centuries later, the Earl of Orrery, writing in 1737, considered that there was:

> *indeed a great Difference in the Complexion of the two Islands.*
> *Nature has been profusely beneficial to Ireland, and Art has been as much*
> *so to England. Here we are beholden to nothing but the Creation; there,*
> *you are indebted to extensive gardeners and costly architects.*[21]

Limerick returned from Italy at much the same time as William Kent, who had spent ten years in Rome studying painting, supplementing his income by acting as a guide and antiques agent for visiting noblemen. Back in England, Kent enjoyed the generous patronage of Robert Boyle, the third Earl of Burlington, whom he had met whilst in Rome. With Burlington's support he established a reputation as a skilled architect, interior decorator and garden designer, rather than as a painter. Horace Walpole said that Kent:

> *was a painter, an architect, and the father of modern gardening. In the*
> *first character, he was below mediocrity; in the second, he was a restorer of*
> *the science; in the last, an original, and the inventor of an art that realizes*
> *painting, and improves nature...He leaped the fence, and saw that all*
> *nature was a garden.*[22]

Thomas Wright was familiar with much of Kent's work in England and was most probably influenced by Kent's ideas for informal gardens which blended with their natural surroundings. Wright has sometimes been acclaimed as the successor to Kent and, after he returned from Ireland, he stepped in to complete Kent's work at Badminton in Gloucestershire when Kent died in 1748. Wright applied many of Kent's ideas and, like Kent, considered the siting of a building every bit as important as its design. This is evident in Wright's numerous sketches and the detailed instructions that accompanied them.[23] The commanding position of Tollymore House was a good example.

Wright's work is often difficult to place in the evolution of the new Gothic style. This is partly because he was such an individualist, and because architecture was but one discipline of this multi-talented man. Professor McCarthy succinctly makes the point that:

> *No specific iconographic or politically-motivated narrative programme seems applicable to any of his work; nor are there literary or heroic or sentimental associations invoked by inscriptions or figural representations. His buildings are quite self-sufficient, interdependent. This is rather exceptional in the period. He seems to have been also uninterested in contemporary publications in Gothic-revival architecture, and one does not find much evidence of interest in real Gothic buildings, though there are sketches of contemporary buildings. This distinguishes him sharply from the second generation of revivalists, especially Walpole.*[24]

The progression from the original plans for Dundalk demesne to those of Tollymore is interesting and mirrors much of what was to happen in garden design. Dundalk was a confined parkland close to the developing town. Wright's original plan, drawn up when he was based at Dundalk, is an example of the formal, Kentian garden enlivened with many of Wright's idiosyncrasies. The topography of Tollymore called for a complete reassessment of the design requirements because the natural features - the river, steep slopes, mountain and sea views - were pre-eminent. The plans for the buildings and parkland would have to complement and play more of a supporting role to the existing, natural features. As Petra Wurz observed in her thesis on Thomas Wright's designs, Dundalk is 'linked with earlier landscape traditions. Its layout reflects the transitional period which is characterised by its mixture of formal and informal elements. Tollymore Park reflects unity, Dundalk variety'.[25] The style of the Dundalk demesne might have been considered rather out of fashion by the end of the 18th century; whereas Tollymore, where the emphasis was on the blending of informal architecture

Dundalk House. Watercolour, artist and date unknown

with natural surroundings, is timeless and never out of step with changes in architectural fashion.

Limerick not only sat in the Irish House of Lords, but represented three English constituencies at Westminster at different times and kept a house at Brook Green in Hammersmith.[26] Wright stayed there on various occasions from 1742 onwards. He also tutored Limerick's relations when in London. It was at this juncture that Limerick prevailed upon Wright to come back with him to Ireland and help with the planning of his Dundalk demesne and Tollymore. However, it was not until the summer of 1746 that the twenty-nine-year-old Wright 'resolved upon a strong invitation to go to Ireland & set out for Parkgate, wate'd 6 days for a wind and at last arrived safe at Dublin'.[27]

Wright stayed just under a year, travelling extensively throughout Ireland. As would be expected, he based himself initially at Dundalk. Limerick's house

'A Survey of the Demesne of Dundalk' by Bernard Scalé, dated 1777

was originally the town's mansion house to which a crenellated, single-storey extension with Gothic windows was added. The plan Wright prepared for the demesne combined formal, axial vistas with serpentine waterways and irregular plantations. Comparing Wright's plan with Scalé's subsequent map, it is apparent that Limerick soon dispensed with much of Wright's formal layout and parterres to the front of the house, preferring lawns, carefully planted trees and screening, not unlike the Delanys' garden at Delville.

While based at Dundalk, Wright was encouraged to visit and record the archaeological and historical remains in the locality. By the autumn of 1746 he, in his own words, 'collected and drew all the plans of *Louthiana*', one of the earliest surveys of this kind. It was published in 1748 and became Wright's most successful publication. Leaving Dundalk, Wright travelled from the Giant's Causeway to Donegal ('Din'd upon ye mountans of Lock Salt in full view of Aragle and Muckish'); and from Limerick ('A fine old fortified town') to

Date-stone on Old Bridge parapet

Dungarvan ('A bleak port').²⁸ It is likely that he prepared the designs for work at Belvedere, south of Mullingar, and Belle Isle near Enniskillen, which he recorded as:

> *a beautiful situation by ye tide. The lake fronting an avenue of islands. Wee saw a buck hunted from ye water follow'd by French horn and many neighbouring gentlemen who all din'd on ye side ye mountain under tents with a great many ladies.*²⁹

Back in Dundalk he began tutoring the young James Hamilton, Limerick's sixteen-year-old son, as well as Lady Limerick and her daughter, the future Countess of Roden. Then, before Limerick had to return to London, Wright went to stay with him at Tollymore for eight days before he left Ireland for good. It had been a whirlwind visit which accomplished more than either party had probably anticipated at the outset. The plans for Dundalk demesne were now well advanced, and the groundwork for Tollymore prepared. This included the design for a house on a prominent position overlooking the river. What is more, Wright had sown enough ideas in the mind of the future second Earl of Clanbrassill for the continuation of the work at Tollymore that would keep him occupied there for the rest of the century. Wright himself was considerably influenced by his experiences in Ireland and what he saw there. His major architectural and

A rustic summerhouse designed by Thomas Wright. *Source: Universal Architecture, 1755*

landscaping undertakings in England were still ahead of him and they generally displayed a far freer style than that shown in the original plans he drew up for Dundalk. Another architect who came to Ireland, Humphry Repton, had much the same experience. He was not employed to do any design work but, by the time he left, had been greatly influenced by the special characteristics of the Irish landscape.[30]

It is not clear how soon after Wright's departure Limerick started work on Tollymore. When Dr Pococke visited Dundalk five years after Wright had left for England, he saw 'fine plantations and walks', with 'a thatched open house supported by the bodies of fir trees' and an artificial, serpentine river with a Chinese bridge.[31] Going on to Tollymore he described how across the river,

> *Lord Limerick has built a thatch'd open place to dine in, which is very Romantick, with a stove near to prepare the Entertainment: above on the North side of this He has begun to build a pretty lodge, two rooms of which are finished, designing to spend the Summer months here.*[32]

The 'thatch'd open place' was probably similar to the one at Dundalk, and they were probably rustic hermitages that were popular at that time.[33] In his instructions for the design of a thatched arbour, Wright specified that the best situation for such a building was on a 'rugged rocky foundation' bordering on a wood and near a river, 'where the approach to it may be made as pleasing as possible'. In another instance he stipulated that 'the situation required of it must be near the sea, or in the neighbourhood of rocks and mountains, the wildest force of nature being the properest accompanyment...'.[34]

This early construction was made of roughly-hewn lumber and thatch with a stone floor. It would have been used for summer afternoon meals with a gathering of friends who had walked down from the main house and across the river, the furniture comfortable but rudimentary, the food brought down and cooked by the servants. Above all, it would have been conducive to good conversation and well-being. Writing in 1748 to Anne Hamilton, the future Countess of Roden, Emily Duchess of Leinster mentioned that, 'you have had charming weather for the Thatched House, I reckon you have dined there almost every day since I last saw you'.[35]

The location of the 'thatch'd house' cannot be identified with absolute certainty, but the probability is high that it was the building marked on both of the Scalé maps as the 'Old Hermitage'. The site lies close to Foley's bridge and is roughly adjacent to the site of the mill-ponds built in the early 19th century to power the sawmill nearby. The Old Hermitage does not appear on any subsequent maps, which indicates that it was not of a very solid construction. Close by is a group of remarkable silver firs (*Abies alba*), known as the Seven Sisters; these are some of the largest recorded in Ireland and would appear to date from the 1780s.[36] Time and gales have since taken their toll, but the name offers a tantalising clue. It has nothing to do with a large family of spinsters, but is the common name given to the seven largest stars in the Taurus constellation, known as the Pleiades. This is derived from the Greek word 'plein' meaning 'to sail'. The ancient Greeks considered navigation safe at the rising of the constellation, and its setting marked the closing of the sailing season. While there are many other interpretations of the figure seven, in landscaping and elsewhere, the association with Wright's navigational expositions is enticing. In many of his landscapes he would plant out trees, or design gardens, according to an astrological formula. It was as if he wished to leave a trademark for posterity. His pupils would have been well aware of this idiosyncrasy.

Another defining feature of Wright's architectural work was the canted bow-window designed to take in all quarters of the sun.[37] The new house, which in 1752 had just two rooms completed according to Dr Pococke, faced south towards the river. The principal section comprised a five-bay, two storey structure, the centre of which consisted of a three-sided bow. On either side of the centre section were two round-headed doorways. In all the later, elaborate additions and alterations, this simple bow-window remained the central feature of the house.

Family records put the start of the house at 1730, two years after Limerick's marriage. But this date has not been substantiated, and is unlikely even with someone of Limerick's energy. Dundalk had priority, being now the family's main residence, and as the architectural features of Tollymore House are closely associated with work subsequently done by Wright in England, they are unlikely to have pre-dated Wright's visit.[38] The first map to show the new 'pretty lodge' is Scalé's version of 1760; the house was not included on James Kennedy's map of 1755. The evidence suggests that Dr Pococke was correct. The completion of this summer residence marked the summit of Limerick's major construction work at Tollymore. From then on he concentrated on planting trees and shrubs, amongst his other activities.

At Westminster, Limerick was one of the Whigs who opposed his friend's father, Sir Robert Walpole. Walpole had come to prominence in 1720 following the South Sea Company scandal, which he denounced, but in the end made a useful profit out of it for himself. As Prime Minister he brought order to the country's finances, kept England out of European squabbles and avoided undue controversy wherever possible. Through careful manipulation, Walpole was responsible for a colourless but remarkable period of peace. Land tax was reduced to a shilling and trade flourished. Finally, outmanoeuvred by people who resented his monopoly of power, he transferred to the House of Lords as the Earl of Orford. Charges of bribery were brought against him, and a Committee of Investigation was appointed in 1742 with Limerick as its chairman. As it happened, no substantive evidence could be uncovered, and proceedings were eventually dropped.

Another landmark in Limerick's political career was his attempt in 1757 to carry a Bill through Parliament for the registration of priests and the establishment of a training college for the clergy. In a letter to supporters he said: 'I have long wished for an opportunity to reconcile, if possible, the Papists in this Country to our happy Constitution, and their own true interest, and to turn a loose, indiscriminate, illegal Connivance into a regular, restrained, legal Toleration'. The Bill passed the Commons but was rejected by the Privy Council. Limerick had visited numerous religious institutions when on the Continent. In one convent, at Oclivellas in Spain, he found 'a great deal of liberty', where the nuns were allowed 'to keep as many servants as they please' and 'most of them have lovers and they frequently dine with company at the grate'. He had also met

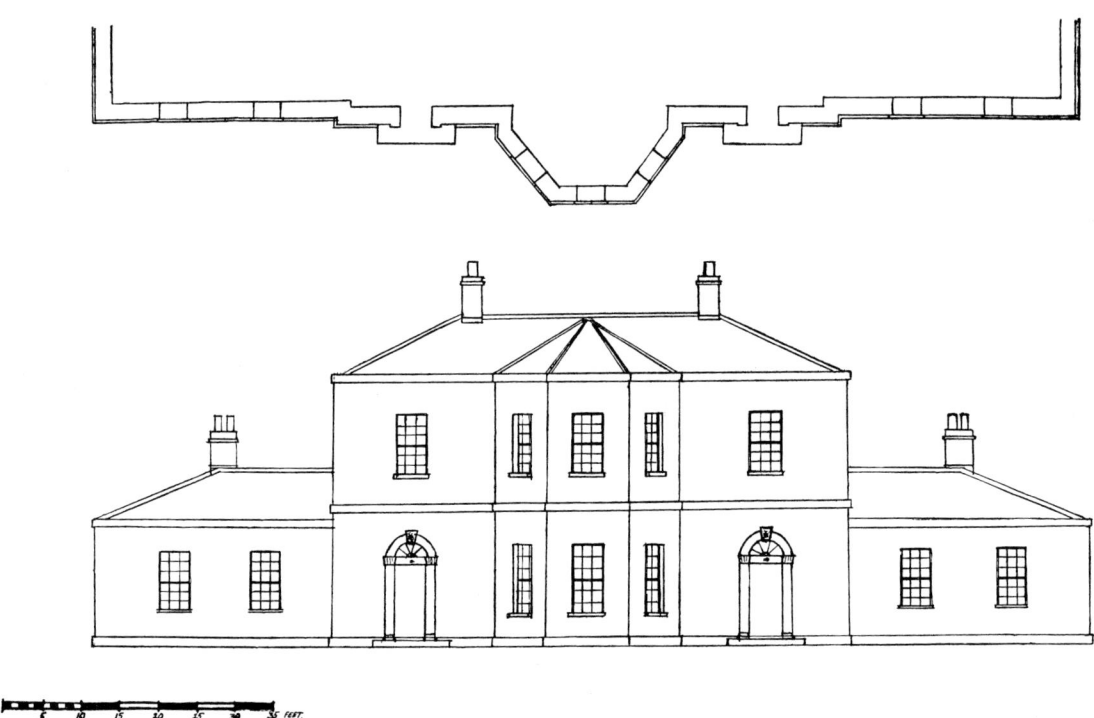

Conjectural drawing of the main block's south elevation as it was originally built

the Curia whilst in Rome and, through his family's connections, was well aware of what was happening in Holland. Though the home of William of Orange, and a divided society, it led the way in the regularization of the priesthood. However, opposition from various quarters was too great for Lord Limerick's Bill, and it would take many generations and much bitterness before his proposals were brought to fruition.

The one area where he was more successful was in the setting up of a Free School in Dundalk, following his mother's earlier initiative. The property was subsequently bought by the Dundalk Council and was until recently the Louth County Library. The proceeds from the sale were invested in the Lord Limerick Trust, which continues to endow secondary schools in the town to this day.

In the mid-18th century, when Tollymore was emerging from a source of high quality venison to a demesne in its own right, the British Empire was expanding from its toe-hold in India; most of Canada had been prised from French control, while further south the youthful energies of the American colonists were quickly realising their strengths and potential. The last of the thirteen colonies to be formed was Georgia. An English philanthropist concocted the idea of emptying

Engraving by Thomas Milton of 'Tullymore Park', after John James Barralet.
*Source: Collection of Select Views from Different Seats of the Nobility and Gentry* (1783-93). This plate was published in 1787

the English prisons of small debtors and re-settling them in the broad expanse of the southern territories. Lord Limerick was one of the original Trustees of the Council of Georgia, but it was not a successful venture. The settlers were probably not the most reliable of citizens in the first place and soon quarrelled amongst themselves, so much so that the Trustees cancelled the charter and Georgia came under the control of the Crown.[39]

However, Limerick's involvement had its rewards. Through his friends in the Americas and various business agents, he sought out plants and seeds for his properties. John Ellis, who had been appointed agent in London for the Irish Linen Board, regularly supplied him with trees and plants. An old friend, Colonel Martin, settled in Antigua from where he sent trees for the demesnes and shells for Lady Limerick's shell-house at Dundalk. Sir Charles Coote of

Cootehill, where Thomas Wright had stayed on his tour of Ireland, supplied Limerick with:

> *every different sort of cherries I have. They certainly come to great perfection here and I believe we have six or seven very different kinds. One of them, marked The Large Black Cherry, exceeds all others I ever saw for its size, tenderness and masses of juice.*

In 1752 Limerick acquired his first consignment of cedars of Lebanon, thus commencing what is today the oldest surviving tree collection in Ireland. These particular cedars, which have long since died,[40] were obtained from a Mr Turner, along with directions how to manage 'the young pine plants my gardener having drawn it up' and noting that if he had any doubts, he was to 'let me know, and I will immediately endeavour to clear them up, but the great question is certainly well answered, the young plants must be plunged in during the winter'.[41]

In those days, seeds were not always easy to source. Ellis wrote in 1757 that he was sorry to report that:

> *the supply of Foreign seeds, which I intended for your Lordship this year, in one New York ship and two Carolina ships, are all lately taken. Insurance from North America is risen to 20 guineas percent prepaid for a cargo of flax seed from Philadelphia and we are afraid that it will be 45 percent. They say the French intend to send all their small men-of-war to cruise on us and ruin our trade and they think it is a better method of affecting us than an invasion.*[42]

Possibly recalling his visit to Fontainebleau, Limerick ordered a consignment of ornamental fish:

> *I have shipped on board the Judith of Newry thirteen China fish and put them into an earthenware jar in a basket with straw about it, and a net over them, with a spigot and faucet to draw water every day and have given the captain written instructions how to treat them during the voyage.*[43]

Ellis also arranged for magnolias to come from the Carolinas, 'the most beautiful plants of our colonies in North America'. He went on to explain how he was 'at the fountain head of all the new discovered plants. I shall always have it in my power to furnish your Lordship with what is new and rare'. Ellis was also pleased to learn that his seeds had thrived, knowing that 'a great deal depends on a gardener who takes delight in his business. Mr Warren informs me your Lordship has got a very good one'.[44]

In 1756 Viscount Limerick was created Earl of Clanbrassill, but by now he had retired from public life. Writing to Colonel Martin in Antigua to thank him for a 'beautiful collection of shells' and a consignment of 'green pines' he mentioned that, 'as to my own particular case prudence, reason and duty to my friends require that I should attend to my private affairs and put an end to my political windmills' adding that 'you will therefore not wonder that I choose to confine myself to ye gentler scenes of rural and domestic life'.[45] But he liked to entertain his friends and enjoyed their company. His wine bills from his French agent bear this out, but above all his favourite pastime was the development of his new demesne. Writing to an old acquaintance he said:

> *I have spent this season in planting, and feel my taste for a country life grow so strong that I think nothing but the pleasure of conversing with my friends will be able to draw me from it, since I have found all my schemes for the Publick to be no better than waking dreams. I must not wish you shou'd fall into the same way of thinking, but if ever you shou'd you will find it affords the soundest of pleasures.*[46]

In this he shared the same aspirations as Thomas Jefferson, the American version of an enlightened 18th-century gentleman who, midway through his Presidency, wrote that 'no occupation is so delightful to me as the culture of the earth, and no culture to that of the garden'.[47]

Limerick may have felt disillusioned with public life towards the end, but he was a man with generally liberal views well ahead of his time who had achieved much. His retreat to a 'country life' was merited. He had set Dundalk on the road to being a prosperous and industrialized town. The foundations of the Tollymore demesne had been laid, and his plantations would grow to the benefit of future generations. It would now be up to his successor to continue the work there.

When he died in March 1758, he left behind his wife, his son James, who became the second Earl of Clanbrassill, and his daughter Anne who had married Lord Jocelyn six years previously. Viscount Jocelyn, eldest son of the Chancellor of Ireland, was created Earl of Roden in 1771. Harriet, Lady Limerick, resided in a house outside Dublin from 1770 and there established a fine collection of trees and shrubs; she died in 1786, the same year as Thomas Wright.[48]

1. A James Hamilton, possibly Viscount Limerick, is known to have been in Padua in 1716.
2. Among the new developments he instigated in the town, Viscount Limerick was instrumental in starting up the cambric (fine linen) industry in Dundalk. He raised money for it, and brought over Huguenot weavers from France to help with the venture. It was the forerunner to the linen industries in places like Lisburn and Lurgan, but never quite so successful.
3. The layout of associated roads, notably the Hilltown and Bryansford Roads, might suggest that they are contemporary with the park, c.1710-15. The building of Bryansford church in 1712 may also have formed part of the same grand plan.
4. The accounts have payments to Mr Keowen 'mason work at ye Deer park wall' £6.6.2 (June 25th 1740); Keowen for 'mason work at ye Deer park wall' £4.13.0 (October 3rd 1740); Andrew Killen 'for jobs in and about the Deer park' £1.12.4½; John Doran for 'several jobs about ye Deer park', £1.5.9; Richard Pray 'for mason work at the Deer park' £1.8.10; William Steel for 'mason work at the Deer park', £1.5.10 and £1.7.8 (including 'oates for the deer'); Robert McGowen for 'nails iron &c for ye Deer park door' £0.7.8 (November 10th 1740). The Skillens (Killen) were a family of renowned stone-masons who continued to build walls in the Mournes for generations. The most impressive work in which they were involved is the Mourne Wall enclosing the Silent Valley. Members of the family still live close to Tollymore.
5. Payment of 16s dated 28th November 1740 made to 'McGrana's Hram for loss of ground taken from him by the new Deerpark and given to the Lord Hillsborough in Exchange for ground got from him for one year ending at May 1740'.
6. W. Harris (1744) *op.cit.*, p82.
7. *Richard Pococke's Irish Tours* (ed. J. McVeagh, 1995), p31-2
8. For a description of this bridge see Gazetteer No.18. The bridge is called 'Strange's Bridge' on the OS 1859 map, after Strange Jocelyn, the younger son of the third Earl of Roden, who subsequently became the fifth Earl of Roden.
9. John Cunningham's statement of account 22.11.1728.
10. Hans Bentinck, Harriet's uncle, was a close personal friend and confidant of William III. He was present at the Battle of the Boyne. As a result, a number of King William memorabilia found their way to Tollymore.
11. Colvin (1995) *op.cit.*, p1100.
12. These early years saw the development of Wright's ideas on astronomy and philosophical theory, probably stimulated by his visit to Holland. His lasting reputation as an astronomer rests on his explanation of the milkiness of the Milky Way, or Galaxy, which is an irregular, but encircling, multitude of stars so distant as to appear almost blended together.
13. At Beaumont Lodge (Old Windsor), Berks, he designed a new house (possibly not executed) for the Dowager Duchess of Kent in 1743; Colvin (1995) *op.cit.*, p1100.
14. Wright is believed to have completed the south (Gothic-style) range of Bishop Auckland Castle, Co. Durham, for John Egerton, ca.1771.
15. G. Allen (1793). 'A sketch of the character of Thomas Wright'. *The Gentleman's Magazine*, pp9-12; 14-15.
16. In particular William Kent, whose landscape designs adapted Claude's technique of

extending the scene by planes through near, middle and far distances to infinity. J.D. Hunt (1987) *William Kent. Landscape Garden Designer,* pp41-2.

17. A. Pope (1731) 'Of Taste; An Epistle to the Earl of Burlington', in *The Correspondence of Alexander Pope*, (ed. G. Sherburn) 1956, vol. II, pp50-52.
18. Malins and Glin (1976), *op.cit.*, p34-6.
19. Edward Walpole continued his association with Ireland, becoming Chief Secretary for Ireland (1737-9). Although he died unmarried, he left three illegitimate daughters, all of whom married well. His second daughter, Maria, became the Duchess of Gloucester.
20. Horace Walpole, fourth Earl of Orford (1717-97). Walpole rather unflatteringly once described Viscount Limerick as 'a pale ill-looking fellow with a bent brow, a whoreson voice and a dead eye of saffron hue'. Johnston-Liik (2002), *op.cit.*, vol. IV, p343.
21. Letter to Tom Southerne dated 28 May 1737 in the Orrery Papers (Harvard College Ms) as quoted in Malins and Glin (1976), *op.cit.*, p2.
22. M.I. Wilson (1984). *William Kent. Architect, Designer, Painter, Gardener, 1685-1748.*
23. Eileen Harris (1971) 'Architect of rococo landscapes: Thomas Wright. III'. *Country Life*, vol. CL (No.3874) Sept 9th, pp.612-615.
24. M. McCarthy (1987). *The Origins of the Gothic Revival.*
25. P. Wurz (1997). An aspect of Irish landscape gardening in the 18th century: Thomas Wright of Durham and his designs for the demesnes of the Earls of Clanbrassil. Thesis for Masters Degree at Sotheby's Institute.
26. Viscount Limerick represented Wendover (1727-34 and 1735-1741); Tavistock (1742-47) and Morpeth (1747-1754). Johnston-Liik (2002), *op.cit.*, vol. IV, p342-3.
27. T. Wright 'The Journal of Thomas Wright, Author of Louthiana [1711-1786]'. J. Buckley (ed.), 1909. *County Louth Archaeological Journal*, II (No.2), pp165-185. Thomas Wright's journal is a brief, but candid aide-mémoire, largely written in the third person.
28. T. Wright (1909) *op.cit.*, pp165-185.
29. Wright is considered responsible for the design for a Gothic tower and a thatched hermitage (both no longer there) at Belle Isle - what Arthur Young referred to as a 'temple built on a gentle hill'. He may have designed the rustic arbour (since rebuilt) at Florence Court, while the work in his style at Belvedere consists of a Gothic arch and the Jealous Wall, the latter being the largest Gothic folly in Ireland. The Gothic arch was illustrated in Wright's *Universal Architecture*.
30. S. Daniels (1999) *Humphry Repton: Landscape Gardening and the Geography of Georgian England*, pp32-3. In 1783, following the granting of legislative independence, Repton accepted a place in the Lord Lieutenant's office in Dublin.
31. *Richard Pococke's Irish Tours* (ed. J. McVeagh, 1995), p30. Writing to Anne Hamilton, the future Countess of Roden, Emily Duchess of Leinster said: 'the description Mr Etables gave me of the Thatched House Viscount Limerick has made at Dundalk is very pretty. I can easily imagine how it looks because he tells me it is very like one in the wood at Goodwood and has a kitchen underground like that' (13.8.1747). The Duchess duly had a thatched house built for herself at Carton.

32. *Richard Pococke's Irish Tours, op.cit.*, p31-2.
33. For example, the hermitage built by the Earl of Orrery at Caledon in the 1740s, see Malins and Glin (1976), *op.cit.*, p46.
34. T. Wright (1755-8) *Universal Architecture - Book I. Six Original Designs of Arbours* and *Book II. - Six Original Designs of Grottos*.
35. The Roden Papers: Letters from the Duchess of Leinster to The Hon. Miss Hamilton, afterwards Countess of Roden, 1745-1774.
36. J.C. Loudon's comments (see Appendix 5) suggest 1784. Ring counts from stumps made in 2004 suggest 1788 (Michael Lear, *personal communication*). It is interesting to speculate that these trees and stumps present in 2004 are a link with Thomas Wright or perhaps more likely planted by Clanbrassill soon after Wright's death in 1786 in commemoration of him.
37. Eileen Harris (1971) 'A flair for the grandiose. The architecture of Thomas Wright. II'. *Country Life*, vol. CL (No.3873), Sept 2nd, pp.546-550. The half-octagon is a Palladian feature, as at Isaac Ware's Wrotham Park; it was adopted in Ireland from the 1740s. Maurice Craig (1976) *Classic Irish Houses of the Middle Size*, pp13-15.
38. The work in England that follows the design of Tollymore is the Menagerie at Horton House, Northamptonshire. It was completed for the second Earl of Halifax around 1754, six years after Wright left Ireland. There is a datestone in the garden at Tollymore inscribed '1726' but it is not certain what this stone represented; but see Chapter 2, note 23.
39. The Dupont Museum in Winterthur, Delaware, USA has a fine portrait of the Trustees, including Viscount Limerick, negotiating with the leader of the Yamacraw Indians.
40. The oldest cedar of Lebanon presently growing at Tollymore is the one in the corner of the car park and dates from 1850 (Michael Lear, *personal communication*).
41. Mr H. Turner to Viscount Limerick (9.10.1757).
42. Mr J. Ellis to Viscount Limerick (5.4.1757). None of these magnolias from the Carolinas were still growing at Tollymore in 2004 (Michael Lear, *personal communication*).
43. Mr J. Ellis to Viscount Limerick (20.1.1756).
44. Mr J. Ellis to Viscount Limerick (5.4.1757). Mr Samuel Warren was Viscount Limerick's Irish agent.
45. Viscount Limerick to Col. Martin in Antigua (31.7.1748).
46. Viscount Limerick to Lord Baltimore (9.1.1747).
47. From a Thomas Jefferson letter quoted in a *Financial Times* article titled 'The president gardener' by Justin Cartwright.
48. She lived at Cypress Grove, outside Dublin. According to J.C.Loudon, who derived his information from James MacKay, Curator of the Botanic Gardens at Trinity College, 'the Dowager Lady Clanbrassill' resided at Cypress Grove 'from 1770 to 1790 [sic], during which period she received a number of foreign trees and shrubs from her son…the collection is numerous and some of the specimens have attained a considerable size. Robinia Pseud-Acacia is 60 ft. high. Laurus nobilis, 30 ft; Juglans regia 70ft; Carpinus Betulus, 90 ft; Quercus Cerris, 70 ft; and Juniperus viriginiana, 40ft., &c'. Loudon (1844) *Arboretum at Fruticetum Britannicum*, vol. I, p111.

*CHAPTER 4*

# The Clanbrassill Era

James Hamilton, the second Earl of Clanbrassill, was twenty-eight when his father died. From his father he inherited an interest in travel, collecting fine art, tree-planting and construction work. What he did not share with his father was a diplomacy in dealing with others, being notoriously stubborn and perhaps sometimes given to melancholy. Furthermore, unlike his father, he was more interested in the political control of Dundalk and the sinecures that went with it, than in the ongoing development of the town. This brought him into conflict with a section of the townspeople who endeavoured, unsuccessfully as it turned out, to wrest this control from the family.[1] Like his father, he studied law for a time and was recorded as being a Brother at the King's Inns.[2] However, his interest in law and politics, whether in England or Ireland, was lukewarm. Emily Duchess of Leinster wrote of the twenty-year-old year old Clanbrassill:

> *I admired his person as I always did but don't think him half so handsome with his hair curled up and powdered as it used to be formerly when it was quite wild and rough, not that I should like to have him wear it so now as I don't like anything that is very particular in dress. As for his manner he is polite, well bred, influenced by others, a little shy.*[3]

Mrs Delany, a person well-known for her forthright views, wrote about Clanbrassill, by now forty-four and about to be married to Grace Foley[4]: 'He and I enter'd into a great deal of Irish talk; he looks old for his age, having lost all his fore teeth, but he is tall, genteel and very well bred, and the evening past very well'. They found they had much in common and in the following year Mrs Delany remarked 'I like him mightily; he is good humour'd, easy and deep in search of botany, which has afforded an ample field of conversation'.[5] If his business dealings left something to be desired, it is on his creative work at Tollymore and his eclectic fine art collection that posterity will judge him more favourably.

Half-length portrait in pastel of James, second Earl of Clanbrassill. By Jean-Etienne Liotard and dated 1774

His father had completed most of the Dundalk demesne, so there were few opportunities for any major new major works, apart from generally enhancing the gardens. Where Clanbrassill had a chance to leave his own mark was at Tollymore. The topographical draftsman Bernard Scalé completed his first map of Tollymore in 1760, two years after Lord Limerick died, so it is possible to assess just how far the demesne had developed under his stewardship.[6] The main house is shown as a simple lodge with its south-facing bow-window. The Barn is there, but without its spire or adjoining archway. The kitchen gardens, and what were to become the Pleasure Grounds to the west of the house, are marked as Nurseries. Spanning the main river is just one bridge, the Old Bridge, leading to the Old Hermitage and plantations. However, another bridge, the New Bridge, crosses the Spinkwee River where the Altavaddy Bridge is today. A huntsman's

CHAPTER 4

Portrait of James, second Earl of Clanbrassill with his hunter 'Mowbray'. Painted by George Stubbs and dated 1769

house and garden are on the same slope above where the lake stands today. Roads are depicted as being completed on the south side of the river towards what is now Parnell's Bridge and eastwards towards the Newcastle entrance. Only two roads work their way uphill, one beside the Spinkwee River and one diagonally from the huntsman's house to the mountain, parallel to the Spinkwee River. There are no follies or substantial gate lodges marked on the map. It is essentially a large deer park with a self-contained sporting residence.

Some of the building work at Tollymore is hard to date with certainty. Bernard Scalé's second map of 1777, seventeen years later, shows only the alteration to the main house and the appearance of the gardens between the Barn and the Hilltown road. The walled-in area of the Pleasure Grounds is now shown as a plantation. Assuming Scalé recorded everything that was there, the greater part of the building at Tollymore took place in the last twenty years of Clanbrassill's

Detail of 'A Survey of Tollymore Park' by Bernard Scalé, 1777

CHAPTER 4

'A Survey of Tollymore Park' by Bernard Scalé, dated 1777

Late 18th-century engraving of the Cascades on the Spinkwee River

life, in the period after he had ceased to sit as an MP in Westminster.[7]

Some of the remaining work was carried on after the earl's death in 1798. His sister, the Countess of Roden, who subsequently took over Tollymore, along with their mother, are shown in Thomas Wright's journal as pupils he tutored in Dundalk. His mother wrote to her brother-in-law, the second Baron Godolphin, to thank him for securing a parliamentary seat for her son and went on to discuss their respective building activities. 'It is mighty pleasant to have work going on in the Country, particularly when it is what will contribute to one's conveniency. I have often dabbled in mortar'.[8] Clanbrassill was not the only builder in the family.

Horace Walpole contended that an owner of a property is the one person best suited to carry out his own improvements:

*He knows where beauty will not clash with convenience, and observes in his silent walks, or accidental rides, a thousand hints that must escape*

> *a person who in a few days sketches out a pretty picture, but had not the leisure to examine the details and relations of every part.*[9]

Thomas Wright was not a conventional, contracting architect, especially as far as his work in Ireland was concerned. He would discuss a project with an owner and prepare sketches for it, but the work would have to be done by the owner himself, using what local craftsmen he could enrol. It was therefore quite possible that the finished work would differ from Wright's conceptual drawings. Although no evidence exists, it must be presumed that Thomas Wright and Clanbrassill continued to exchange ideas concerning the building works at Tollymore. Apart from the finely cut stone of the Bryansford Gate and Clanbrassill's Barn, much of the work at Tollymore was of a slightly coarser construction than that associated with Wright's later work in England. Wright also favoured the use of local materials, where possible, and he would have impressed this on his Irish clients. It would explain the exceptional use of the granite bap-stones brought up from the river and either used whole or split on site by the stone-masons. Mourne granite was available in abundance for the finer work, and there was no shortage of rough shale that could be quarried as and where needed. Not far from the Barbican are the remains of an old limekiln which would have supplied much of the lime mortar needed for the building work.

Wear, tear and generations of neglect have taken their toll on the remaining buildings at Tollymore.[10] When first constructed, some of the buildings, such as the Horn Bridge and the Barbican, would have been lightly rendered and may even have been painted with a coloured wash. Glin Castle in County Limerick is an example of this style and finish. What is seen today is just the base rendering and, in some instances, even this has weathered away, or been gouged out by vegetation.

The second Earl of Clanbrassill's first priority at Tollymore was the alteration to the main house, which he completed some time before 1777. Three sides were added, thereby enclosing a courtyard to the rear of the house. It must have presented an unusual appearance. The entire addition was a simple, single-storey structure, but each side had a length of nearly 40 metres. Only his father's centre section was two-storey. It is likely that Clanbrassill designed the extensions himself and used local craftsmen to complete the work. With its low-slung addition and commanding central edifice, it may have looked incomplete. The *Dublin Penny Journal* in 1834, however, considered that it had the appearance of an 'elegant cottage', while the much travelled Rector of Clonenagh, the Rev. Daniel Augustus Beaufort, expressed rather mixed views on the building after

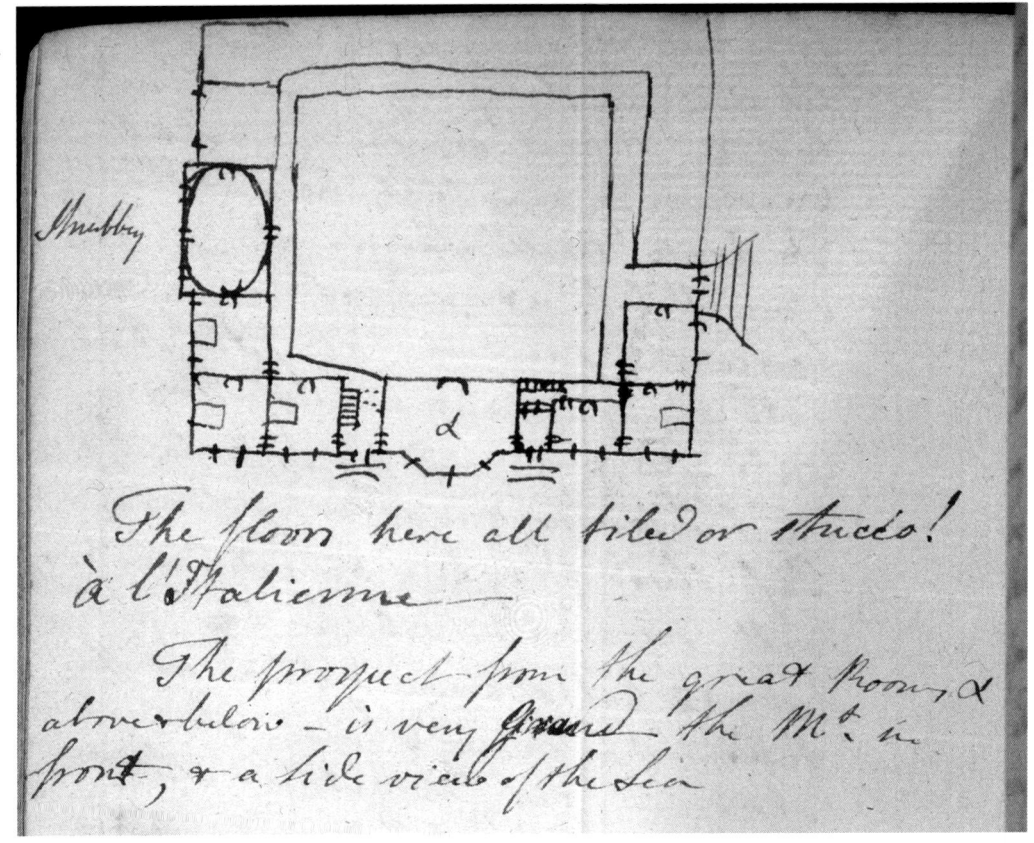

The Rev. Beaufort's sketch plan of the house. *Source: TCD, Ms. 4028 fol. 65v*

his visit in 1787:

> The house, of which only the centre is two storeys high, is built round a large court and contains some very fine rooms, but too many long cold passages in the windows of which are a great many designs of painted Glass, mostly Flemish.[11] The floors here all tiled or stucco à l'Italienne.[12]

A little sketch done by Beaufort during his visit shows the main entrance switched to the east wing. The front rooms are bedrooms and in the west wing is an oval drawing room. The entrance to the courtyard is not marked, but at a subsequent date it was from the north side. In the same year, Thomas Milton published an engraving after J.J. Barralet (see page 41), together with a similar account of the building:

> 'Though not lofty in itself, it is extensive having four fronts, enclosing a square area; each part is different from the rest'.[13]

The redeeming feature of the house was its position. It was built at the top of a slope some 75 metres above the river. As Beaufort recorded, 'The prospect from the great Rooms & above & below - is very grand - the Mt in front, & a side

South front of the house looking across the lawn with the Horn Bridge in the foreground, circa 1865

view of the Sea'. Lord Limerick with advice from Thomas Wright had chosen the site well. But the new addition to the house did not last that long. The low elevation invited a second storey and duly got one in the next century. However, the ground floor plan, including the oval room, was retained to the end.

Originally, the main avenue ran not through the Bryansford Gate, or the Barbican, but from what is now the West, or Hilltown Gate, close to the present Mountain Centre. As Dundalk was the family's main residence, the usual approach would have been from the Hilltown direction. The second Scalé map of 1777 shows a porter's lodge at the western end with an avenue meandering through the upper part of the demesne towards the house. There are no records of this early lodge and it may have been a relatively basic structure. However, with the work on the main house now complete, Clanbrassill could turn his attention to new entrance gates. Besides the Western Avenue, there were three other routes into the demesne, from Bryansford on the north, the Newcastle road on the

Proposal for 'Gothic Watergate over a Canal' from the Thomas Wright Album. *Source: Avery Architectural and Fine Arts Library, Columbia University. Drawings from this album appear to date from around 1768-1770*

east and a gateway lying south of the river on the east side. While two of these entrances would wait for another generation, both the Bryansford and Barbican Gates would allow full rein to Clanbrassill's architectural exuberance.

Gate lodges built in the 18th century were a highly distinctive class of architecture in their own right, and could only have been built in a time of relative peace; otherwise they would not have survived. Besides providing an entrance to a demesne, with usually a porter in attendance, gate lodges announced to all and sundry the tastes and character of the owner, and the first impression he wanted to convey to prospective visitors. They were the overtures to the demesne and intended to create an inquisitiveness for what lay ahead. Irish gate lodges were not restrictive entrances to parkland beyond; a stout boundary gate would have done the job to greater purpose, as indeed was sometimes the case. They were opportunities for display, whilst at the same time being in harmony with the demesne lands on the other side.[14] The Barbican and Bryansford Gates are in stark contrast to each other architecturally, yet both meet these criteria.

In the Middle Ages a fortified city protected its main gate with a tower, and

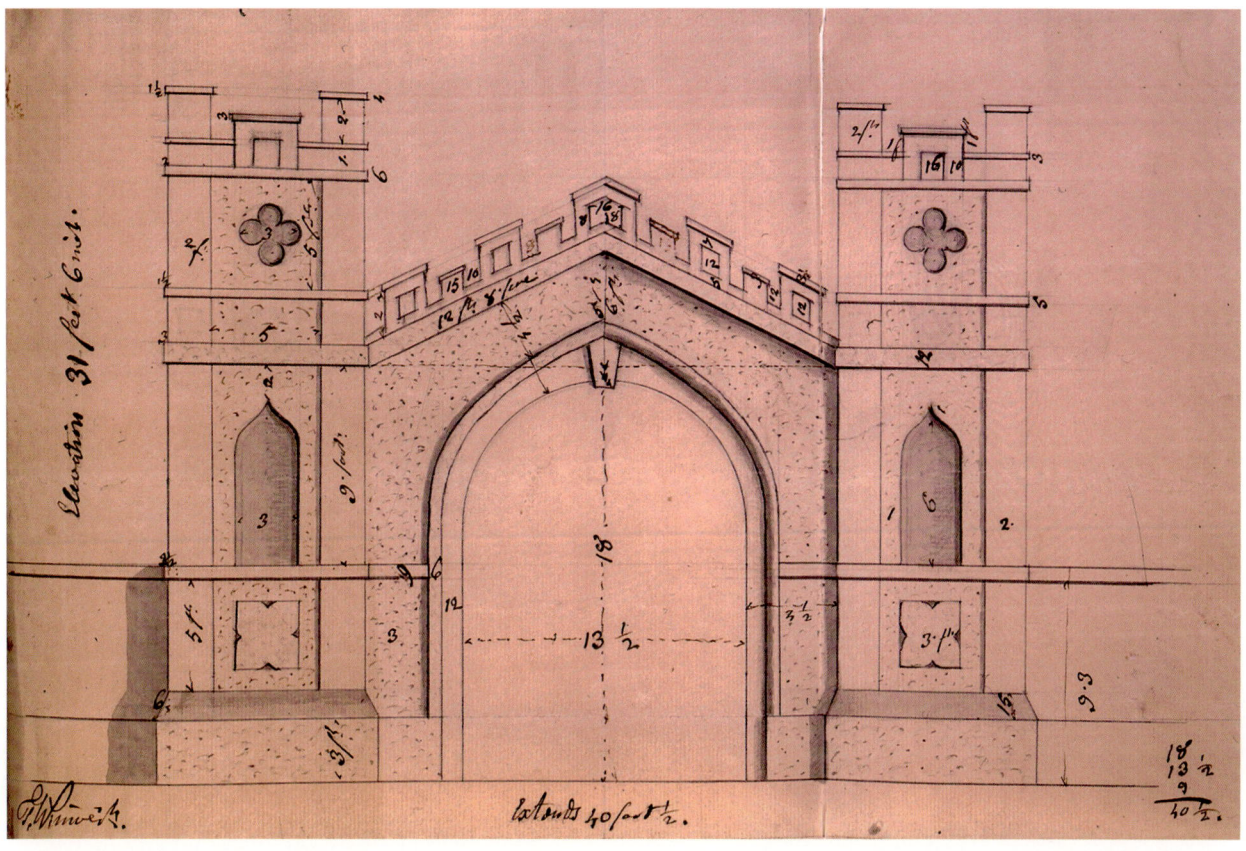

Proposal for a gothic gatescreen from the Thomas Wright Album.
*Source: Avery Architectural and Fine Arts Library, Columbia University*

sometimes a double tower astride the entrance. This key strongpoint was known as a barbican. One such example was the St Laurence Gate in Drogheda. What remained of it after Cromwell's visit to that town was recorded by Wright in *Louthiana*. When turning over ideas for a gate lodge that would be a little out of the ordinary and a light-hearted extravagance, Wright prepared drawings for a barbican gateway that was adapted by Clanbrassill. In due course it would become the main entrance to Tollymore.

Similar gatescreens to the Barbican were also prepared by Wright for other clients; one among his drawings in the Avery Library, Columbia University, entitled 'An Ornamental Gate in the Saxon Stile of Gothick Architecture', may have been intended as a design for the Bishop of Durham's seat at Auckland Castle. Another more elaborate version of the Barbican gate was prepared by Wright for the north gate of Rothley, near Wallington in Northumberland.[15] The basic design was also used by Wright for other building types, for example the gothic summer house at Nuthall Temple, Nottinghamshire, built for Sir Charles Sedley around 1770.

Unlike the Bryansford Gate, the Barbican does not have a view of a valley

A pair of rough sketches for gothic gatescreens from the Thomas Wright Album.
*Source: Avery Architectural and Fine Arts Library, Columbia University*

A pair of rough sketches for rustic follies from the Thomas Wright Album.
*Source: Avery Architectural and Fine Arts Library, Columbia University*

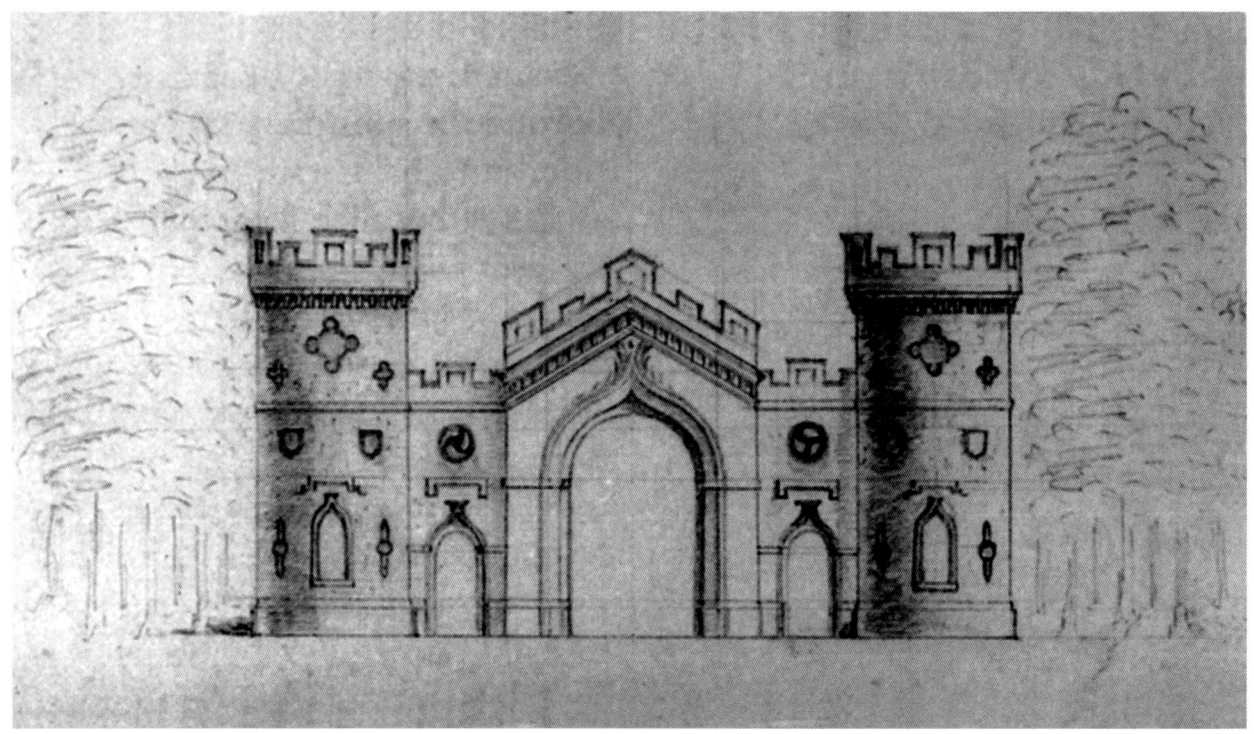

Thomas Wright's design for a gothic gatescreen at Rothley Park, near Wallington, Northumberland, 1769.
*Source: The National Trust, Wallington*

and mountains beyond that has to be taken into consideration. The gate's overall design could, therefore, be a solid statement in its own right. In Clanbrassill's time there was open parkland on the other side of the gate. The Himalayan cedars along the present avenue were planted some time between the Ordnance Survey map editions of 1834 and 1859. First introduced into the British Isles about 1831, these slow-growing and long-lived species can grow to 30m in height in this country, where they were often planted in parks and gardens. They are most beautiful trees, with a somewhat pendent habit, and readily deserve their name *Cedrus deodara*, derived from Devadara – God's tree. Besides being venerated and used in India for construction work, these trees are symbols of perseverance and durability. As stately, spacious trees, they line the Barbican Avenue as far as the eye can see.[16]

The gateway itself is not on the main road but set back a hundred and fifty metres at the end of a slightly upward-sloping avenue of its own framed by beech and lime trees. Once through the gateway, the avenue slopes gently down to a small stream, then up again to follow the contours of the parkland.

The main entrance passes through the centre of the Barbican under a Gothic archway. There are two complementary arches, each on either side, one for pedestrians and the other providing access, via a spiral staircase to the rear,

The west side of the Barbican Gate looking down from the avenue of *Cedrus deodara*

to the battlements above. The two smaller arches are incorporated into round, crenellated towers. The building has two arrow-slits, or quatrefoil loopholes, on either side of the central arch. Each one was cut locally from four granite blocks and built into the random stonework of the walls. Likewise, the towers have blind trefoil reveals, again cut in the same manner. There is evidence of a light rendering, but the loopholes are too flush with the outer surface to carry much mortar. At some point, the building may have had a wash finish. To complete the overall effect, a flag used to fly from a pole on the southern tower.

When the Rev. Beaufort visited Tollymore in 1787, he passed through 'a new handsome Gothic gateway' from Bryansford village. This gate presented an altogether different challenge for Clanbrassill. The avenue drops away almost immediately from the main road. It falls steeply past Clanbrassill's Barn, and one is aware of another, deeper valley before the climb up forested slopes to the mountains above. A solid, castellated gateway would have been out of

The outside (east side) of the Barbican gate, circa 1860

The inside (west side) of the Barbican gate showing the Porter's Lodge on the left, circa 1910. *Source: Folk and Transport Museum, W.A. Green Collection, 1859*

The Bryansford Gate, circa 1860. The fine wrought iron gates had gone by the Edwardian era

place. Instead, Clanbrassill, guided by Wright's suggestions, chose an elegant, light construction for this entrance. The high central arch, fine flying buttresses and pinnacles do not distract from the vista beyond but tend to enhance it. The gateway is an admirable example of the development of well-proportioned Gothic architecture.

Like the Barbican, the Bryansford Gate has a central, vaulted arch, but this time with two side entrances for pedestrians. These entrances pass under matching towers which in turn support the central section. The tops of the side towers are battlemented and have corner pinnacles decorated with small bap-stones. They correspond with similar pinnacles on the main arch. Crocketted pinnacles were often used by Wright and appear on his extensions to the west towers of Durham Cathedral. The spandrels above the main arch have a variation of bap-stone decoration: central stones have three semi-spherical stones radiating from them to the corners of the spandrels. What finally makes the Bryansford Gate particularly appealing and elegant is the use of finely-cut Mourne granite. Flanking one side of the avenue were hornbeams. These were cut down in the 1920s and replaced with cypresses which now lend a rather sombre appearance to

The Clanbrassill Barn and its steeple as seen from the Bryansford Avenue. The Mourne Mountains lie in the distance to the south

the vista. One person not easily impressed by demesnes, other than his own, was Sir Richard Colt Hoare who was clearly influenced by his approach to Tollymore through the Bryansford Gate:

> *Few, if any, noblemen, either in Ireland, or in the sister kingdom, can boast of a residence placed in so singular and romantic situation. The approach to it, under a Gothic gateway, is truly prepossessing.*[17]

Halfway down the avenue, on the right-hand side, Clanbrassill's Barn appears expectantly, but does not intrude into the view of the valley and mountains beyond. Clanbrassill certainly harboured grand ideas for the completion of his 'offices' as estate buildings were then called. He commissioned Robert Adam to design a tower for him (or was sent designs by Robert Adam on the chance of a commission), and it is perhaps fortunate that he backed his own instinct and did not attempt Adam's elaborate structure, which would have been out of keeping with his other work at Tollymore.[18]

CHAPTER 4

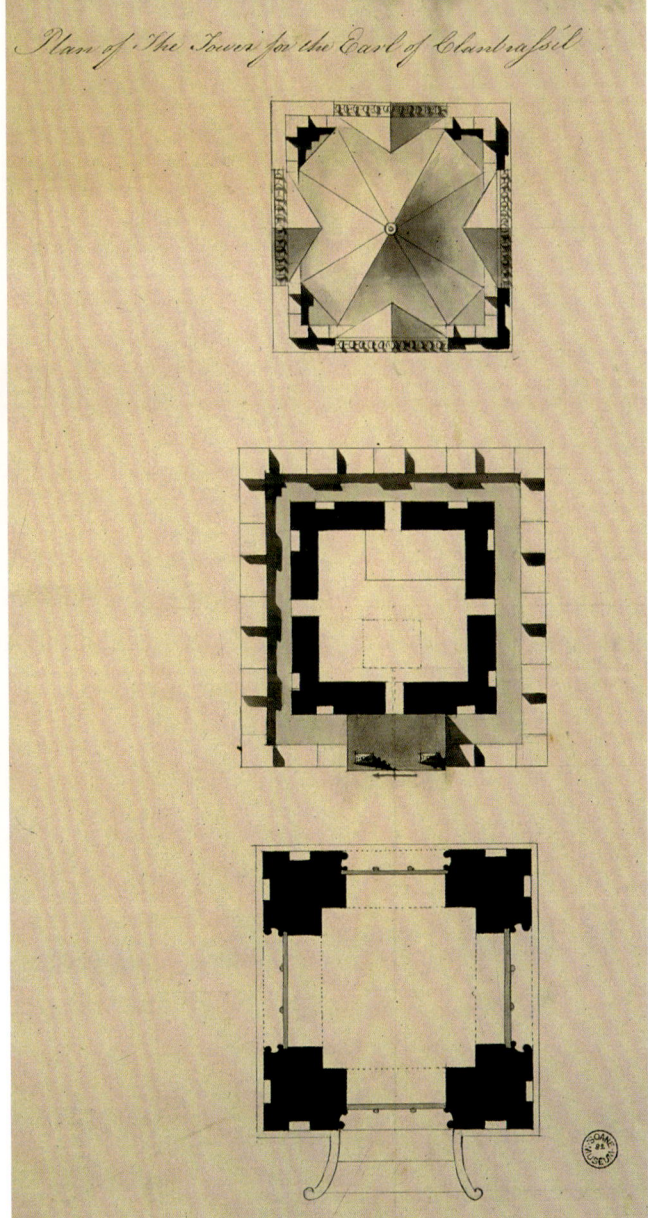

Robert Adam's elevation of a proposed tower and steeple. Probably drawn in 1769.
*Source: Sir John Soane's Museum*

Robert Adam's floor and roof plans of a proposed tower and steeple. Probably drawn in 1769.
*Source: Sir John Soane's Museum*

The Clanbrassill Barn and adjoining arch, post 1955
*Source: Postcard view*

Like his other undertakings at Tollymore, the Barn was almost certainly designed by Clanbrassill in the Thomas Wright style, and constructed by local craftsmen under his supervision. Construction work was evidently underway in 1774, for in that year Clanbrassill's mother wrote to Lord Godolphin concerning her son's political career and in the course of the letter remarked that:

> *My son and his wife stayed longer at Tollymore than I expected, for the bad weather has been a great hindrance to the offices that are now building there, which my son wants to see up before he leaves the place.*[19]

But supervising the works had its hazards. While Clanbrassill was overseeing the quarrying of granite in the mountains for his buildings, a loose boulder became detached and rumbled down towards him. He was able to throw himself to one side, but his foot was caught and crushed. Three surgeons attended him for nearly a month before he was declared to be out of danger.[20]

Clanbrassill's Barn imitates a small-sized Gothic church cleverly disguising the main uses of the building. It was built at around the same time as the Castle Barn at Badmington in Gloucestershire where Wright worked for the Duchess of Beaufort. The main part of the Clanbrassill Barn is made of random local stone, but small slates and flints have been pushed into the pointing to imitate

Detail of the steeple on the Clanbrassill Barn

a medieval building process known as galletting. Archways today sometimes incorporate galletting to allow for the settlement of heavier stones. The windows and doorways are all finished in cut granite, and at each corner of the building are granite pinnacles. At the west end, there is a small bell-cote with a crocketted spire above it. A square platform in two sections rises above the Barn at the avenue end where a sundial is built into the lower section, and the usual bap-stones decorate the upper section. Onto this platform was built an 'octagonal steeple' with openings on each face. Around the fringe of the 'octagonal steeple' are eight slender granite pinnacles. The granite spire, surmounted by the inevitable bap-stone, forms a base for the weathercock. In 1785 Rudhall of Gloucester built a clock for the tower, which Clanbrassill records as 'finished 1789'.[21]

At the gable end of his Barn the Earl of Clanbrassill subsequently built a delicate Gothic archway to his offices. It is not a major construction in itself, but a fine example of the Wright/Clanbrassill style. The archway, which complements the Barn, follows a similar pattern in so far as the bases of the arches are square with pointed panels well finished in cut granite. Then, at a higher level, they change to octagons. These are capped by small domes topped by acorn finials fashioned from bap-stones. The acorn is an ancient symbol of longevity and enlightenment.

Clanbrassill wisely confined his construction work in the demesne to buildings that fulfilled a specific purpose and, following his earlier tutoring, did not attempt to compete with the natural attractions of the landscape. On or outside the boundary walls, this was a different matter. On the approach to Tollymore from Hilltown, the first buildings to catch the attention are what are now known as Lord Limerick's Follies. Their date is open to question, but they are of a similar period and construction to the Barbican. All three buildings are very much in the Wright style and those opposite the demesne appear on an estate map dated 1791, where they seem to be painted white.

The first, and largest, marks the boundary with the Marquess of Downshire's property and is close to the original West Gate into Tollymore. It is built on a small knoll, which gives it a more imposing position. A flight of steps reaches a circular base which supports a hexagonal tower. On the central aspect of the tower is a large niche overlooking the road and demesne. The other sides have alternate niches and quatrefoil loopholes. At each corner of the projecting stonework above the tower, split stones are stood on end. Above, the centre spire is decorated with three diminishing courses of bap-stones. Apart from marking the estate boundary or gateway to the demesne, or perhaps functioning as a landmark, the

The Hilltown Road with the Hexagonal Tower and an early motor car, circa 1910. *Source: Folk and Transport Museum, W. A. Green Collection, 1831*

exact purpose of the tower remains unknown.

Some 200 metres down the road from the tower, are two rather grand gateposts. Each has a circular pier with a loophole to the front. The piers are capped with a projecting stone course supporting more bap-stones. Small spires then rise from the centre of the piers. Mourne gateposts are usually solid, round structures, but this pair have taken the practice to a new dimension.

On the other side of the road, and 300 metres further on, is a building (see page 191) that is easily passed by and often ignored. Quite different from the previous two structures, it is one of the most perfect examples of Wright-inspired work at Tollymore. It is possible that it might have been a pedestrian entrance gate. The overall composition and proportions mark it out as a small gem of fanciful Gothic architecture (see page 192). Its base is almost a square, with a pointed blind arch on the front elevation. The main cornice above is supported with round stones at each corner and in the middle, similar to the tower further

The Hexagonal Tower on the Hilltown Road

Gate posts on the Hilltown Road

Ruined Arch in the woods

up the road. A four-sided obelisk then rises in two sections to an egg-shaped ovoid stone at its summit. This upper pyramid is decorated with bap-stones, but it is the two round stones on the square base that catch the eye and lend a slightly grotesque air to what would otherwise have been a fairly conventional structure. On either side of the folly, two small flying buttresses join the main building to the demesne wall.

Between the roadside folly and the river, there is an unusual ruin now much overgrown by forest, its Gothic archway terminally weathered and strangled with ivy. Bap-stones were built into the front face and more such stones can be found among the wall debris nearby. Just what its purpose was is another of Tollymore's mysteries. The entrance faces north, away from the river, and it does not command a very prominent position, which suggests that it was not a building of any aesthetic value. Not far from the site, Bernard Scalé's map of 1777 shows a Bullock House, but another clue can be found in a 1920s photograph of

The Laundry with its Wrightian Arch, crow-stepped gable and pinnacle, now demolished. In the foreground are members of the Special Constabulary with their guns and vehicles, probably in 1923

a group of 'B' Special Police in the yard of the main house returning from patrol. In the background is Clanbrassill's Laundry which was demolished along with the main house. The decorated Gothic porch was built in a very similar style and it is possible that the ruin was an agricultural building used in connection with the production of cattle or deer.

Not far from this ruin is the Hermitage, overlooking a long, meandering pool on the Tollymore River. While there is an eremitic tradition in Ireland going back to the early monastic era, which involved retreat to islands and even caves, the hermitages of the 18th century were less penitential. Those designed by Wright and others were principally for enjoyment, while at the same time retaining an air of mysticism and cenobite meditation. In Ireland they acted as places for shelter, contemplation and conversing with friends.[22] On the Continent, and occasionally in England, they went a stage further. In his diary, Lord Limerick recalled seeing the hermitages at Fontainebleau:

> *Louis built three hermitages in the forest, one of them was pulled down by reason of the hermit being murdered there. The other two are still*

The Hermitage. A view from the Pool

*standing both of which I saw. The late King used to give entertainment to the ladies at one of them that is situated in the wildest place that can be imagined.*[23]

The Hermitage at Tollymore, which is six metres above the river, appears to grow naturally out of the rock gorge and is well hidden from either approach. The access is up a flight of stone steps and along a walkway suspended over the river. The main chamber, 3.70m x 2.50m, is built into the rock and has a domed ceiling. There is a stone bench against the back wall, and the alcove above once contained a bust with a Greek inscription commemorating Clanbrassill's friend, the Marquess of Monthermer.[24] The primitive stone composition provides two openings over the river and a continued passageway supported underneath by a rough-built arch. The second chamber is much smaller but built in the same manner. Steps from this section, which is approximately 1.20 metres square, lead up to the beech woods above.

Inscription on the back wall of the Hermitage as copied by Atkinson (1823), p201

ΚΛΑΝΒΡΑΣΣΙΛΛΟΣ
ΜΟΝΘΕΡΜΕΡῼ
ΦΙΛῼ ΗΔΥΤΑΤῼ
ΕΤΕΙ
ΧΓΗΗΗΓΛΛΛ

It is hard not to experience a tangible feeling of tranquillity and peaceful rumination on reaching the Hermitage where the water glides quietly below. The experience is accentuated by the silent forest on the opposite bank and the distant roar of water. It was at the Hermitage more then anywhere else that Clanbrassill demonstrated the importance of Alexander Pope's theory of the 'Genius of Place'. The river, thundering down through a cleft in the rocks into the long placid pool, provided a natural focus which was complemented by the fern-covered stonework of the Hermitage. It is a fitting tribute to his friend who died young and about whom little is known.

In the 19th century, a suspension bridge was thrown across the river just upstream from the Hermitage. Some of the securing points are still in place. The bridge would have obtruded into the setting of the Hermitage, so it is perhaps no loss that it was demolished in 1936 and replaced with a wooden bridge 100 metres downstream, where the water was dammed between piers to provide power for the sawmill. Part of an old sluice-gate and fixtures can still be found there today. [25]

Further downstream, past the Old Bridge built by his father sixty years previously, is Clanbrassill's own architectural jewel, Foley's Bridge. This bridge owes little to the influence of Thomas Wright: it has a closer affinity with an Alpine pack-horse bridge encountered in the Haute-Savoie on the road to Italy. The slender, semicircular arch high above the river supports a gently sloping pathway, which curves outwards at either end. Between the arched underside and the parapet top, a depth of some 1.20 metres, this technically quite sophisticated structure incorporates the wedged-shaped voussoirs of the arch, the parapet with its centre stone and the bap-stone embellishment. The choice of site for

Foley's Bridge, circa 1910. *Source: Folk and Transport Museum, W. A. Green Collection, 565*

a rounded, high-arched bridge is exemplary. It spans the top of a gulch flowing into a deep pool which opens out and mirrors the bridge above. Upstream, the rapids are framed in the curvature of the arch, and the beech trees on either side add to the Arcadian setting, especially when in their autumn colouring.

It is possible that Clanbrassill intended the bridge as an access to the Old Hermitage close to the seven giant fir trees nearby, or perhaps the contour of the river bank at that point just lent itself to a new construction. It has always been supposed that the bridge was dedicated to Clanbrassill's wife, Grace Foley. However, this does not conform with the inscription on the oval stone in the parapet marked 'Ht. Foley'. The Countess of Clanbrassill had two nieces, both of whom were called Harriet, and it is more likely that the bridge was dedicated to one of them. They were both young girls when the bridge was completed in 1787. Perhaps it was intended to mark an important birthday, or a recovery from an illness, but whatever the reason and whoever she was, Ht. Foley had the most beautiful bridge over the river dedicated to her.

Foley's Bridge was not Clanbrassill's only bridge built at Tollymore. Some 500 metres further downstream is the Clanbrassill Bridge, sometimes known as the

Foley's Bridge in the autumn

The centre stone of Foley's Bridge

Clanbrassill (Ivy) Bridge showing its parapets and turrets. *Source: Folk and Transport Museum, W.A. Green Collection, 2*

Ivy Bridge. The style of this bridge was very much influenced by Wright. It was built in the form of a Gothic arch, but given the height and width of the span, it is not the most robust of designs. The bridge has a panel in the parapet inscribed with a 'C' under a coronet, and another opposite dated '1780'. At either end the parapet curves outwards towards four small, well-proportioned turrets. On each side of the turrets are pointed niches. Above these, crennelations surround the central, cut-stone pinnacles. The four turrets share similarities with Lord Limerick's follies on the main road and they can all be linked to drawings made by Wright. In earlier years the bridge stood out and made a statement on its own, but it has subsequently become much entangled with ivy and overshadowed by beech and fir woods, so much so that it cannot be fully appreciated in the way Clanbrassill intended. In the Lawrence Collection in the National Library of Ireland, there is a photograph of yet another suspension bridge downstream from the Clanbrassill bridge but no remains can be found.

There are other bridges on the Tollymore River worthy of note, such as the early Trassey Bridge and the Priest's Bridge, but these are just outside the demesne boundaries. However, one bridge which is very much part of the demesne and built in the Thomas Wright style is the Horn Bridge close to the site of the

One of the Turrets on the Clanbrassill (Ivy) Bridge

main house. According to Scalé's map, the original avenue from the West Gate ran through the Pleasure Grounds and up to the front of the house. Bisecting these grounds was a small stream, which tumbled its way downhill to join the main river above the Old Bridge. With the plantation by the house now growing into an established arboretum, it was time to landscape the stream. Although it would dry out in hot summers, it was carefully banked and the river-bed paved. A walkway accompanied the stream downhill, and the steep slopes on either side presented fine opportunities to create shrubberies and rock gardens. When a new avenue from the West Gate swept round below the house, the chance to build a bridge which passed over both the path and stream presented itself. Wright designed several bridges along the lines of the Horn Bridge, and it is safe to assume that this one can be attributed to his fanciful genius. The central,

The Horn Bridge from the south east. The small bridge beside it is a modern Forest Service construction

pointed arch spans a wooden footway, which in turn provides a passageway over the stream. On either side of the archway are two large, blind quatrefoils and two semi-circular piers rising up to form part of the parapet. Each pier has a recessed niche said to have displayed stags' horns. The bridge was probably built at much the same time as the Barbican and has similarities with its spirited relation. Both are of a more massive composition than the other buildings at Tollymore and bear a close resemblance to Wright's design for the Gothic Arch at Wallington in Northumberland (see page 60).[26]

The Horn Bridge, in full view of the house, divided the walk-way to the main river, lending an unseen depth to the valley below. On the path above the bridge, set in amongst the rhododendrons and azaleas, is a small classical fountain known as the Lion's Mouth.

The Lion's Mouth Fountain in the Pleasure Grounds, circa 1870

Another tributary of the Shimna River, which plunges down the opposite slopes of the valley, is known as the Spinkwee River. Its main waterfall was described in the Ordnance Survey Memoirs for 1834-36 as being:

> ...of about 30 feet. The trees upon the bank, meeting and forming an arch over it, give to it a beautiful appearance....The waterfall is seen to most advantage from an old bastion formed of irregular stones, now overgrown with moss.[27]

As at Powerscourt, the waterfall was a popular destination for a walk. This was a period when leisure, especially for ladies, was a pastime that required serious planning. The top of the Cascade Falls has been slightly altered to make the flow more spectacular and a path built down into the ravine to the 'old bastion' below. The whole design is once again in the spirit of Thomas Wright and may have been drawn up by him when he visited Tollymore in 1746.

By the time Clanbrassill had completed his bridges on the main river, Wright had long since retired to his home at Byers Green near Durham to rebuild his house and 'prosicute' his astronomical studies. His main achievements in building and landscape design were by then behind him.[28] When he returned from Ireland, he had worked for numerous patrons in England, but fashions in landscaping and architecture had begun to change, and new ideas superseded those espoused by Kent and Wright. Capability Brown came to the forefront of landscape design, so much so that Wright found some of his own work torn apart and replaced by Brown, a development he accepted with his usual equanimity. Fortunately, no such changes took place at Tollymore. As a demesne with no deliberate design for its beginning and end, this could easily have been the case. Instead, Clanbrassill remained faithful to his old mentor. One of the later works to be completed in the Wright style, the Bryansford Gate, was finished in 1786, the year Thomas Wright died.

Clanbrassill was not solely interested in construction work at Tollymore. He developed a passion for forestry and was to devote considerable energy to expanding the woodland plantations begun by his father. At that time a number of landowners were developing new techniques in commercial planting and propagation, most notably in Scotland, where coniferous afforestation was taking place on a massive scale. Foremost among these landowners was the fourth Duke of Atholl, who had 'formed ten thousand acres of woodland in the Perthshire highlands by planting 14 million trees [mainly European larch]' between 1774 and 1826.[29] Clanbrassill visited the Duke of Atholl's plantations at Dunkeld in Perthshire and was inspired to adopt similar ideas for planting on his own lands in Ireland.[30]

Loudon in his *Arboretum et Fruticetum Britannicum* believed that Clanbrassill began planting at Tollymore 'about 1770 or perhaps a few years before that period'.[31] This is probably correct as the Dublin Society awarded him a gold medal in 1774 for his tree planting at Tollymore, while previously he had also received a gold medal for planting ash trees at his property in County Meath. The main period of planting at Tollymore, however, seems to have been in the twelve years from 1777, when the earl planted 337,318 trees, as he himself meticulously recorded in his almanac for the year 1789.[32] These were mostly placed in the existing Deer Park, but evidently also included the Curraghard Plantation on the south-east side of the demesne.

The suitability of Tollymore for coniferous trees was remarked upon by Loudon, noting that 'the soil and situation, the first ridge of the Mourne mountains, appear to be particularly suited to the larch and fir'.[33] Among the trees planted at Tollymore between 1777 and 1789 there were 25,478 larch.[34] Silver fir and Scotch pine were also extensively planted, the latter being indicated by the title-page of a treatise published by Clanbrassill in 1783, which reads *An Account of the Method of Raising and Planting the Pinus Sylvestris, that is, Scotch Fir, or Pine, as now Practised in Scotland*.[35] Very few treatises on tree planting were published in 18th-century Ireland, and it is possible that Clanbrassill was encouraged to produce this pamphlet by his first cousin, James Fortescue of Ravensdale Park, Co. Louth, who is generally accepted as the author of a better known treatise published in 1773 entitled *Some Hints on Planting. By a Planter.*[36] Significantly, both works came from the same press, that of the Stevensons of Newry.

Besides directions on planting, Clanbrassill's treatise contains hints on protection from birds, and even the number of trees a person can be expected to plant in a day. He advocated the now accepted method of planting trees close together:

> *In these natural Woods Nature doth the Whole Work and no Gardener comes to trim, prune, or dress them; yet when old, they produce Masts, without a knot; their Thickness makes them shoot up in Height, for their Tops to get to the Air; and each striving to get the highest, carries the Whole along.*

In the course of his planting at Tollymore the earl discovered that larch grown on the north-facing slopes grew slower and produced better timber than elsewhere. It was consequently well suited for ships' planking and spars.[37] Years later in 1844 Loudon verified this view by noting that the larch at Tollymore was:

> *in much estimation for its great tenacity, and it supplies masts of from 50 ft. to 60ft. in length. As a selection from a great number, we take, one tree, which at 80 years of age is 84 ft. high…another tree, at 60 years of age, is 66ft. high…The larch…is grown on the side of a steep hill facing north, on a stiff gravelly substratum, which corresponds with the natural situation in which the larch is found in Switzerland…and with the situations in the neighbourhood of Dunkeld, where the best larch is grown*

*by the Duke of Athol… Monteath, the Scottish forester, we are informed by Lord Roden,… considers the Tollymore larch to be very superior in quality to the generality of the Scotch or Welch larch.*[38]

Not everyone at that time necessarily approved of the new ideas of planting coniferous monoculture forests. When Sir Richard Colt Hoare, the owner of the famous landscape park at Stourhead, visited Tollymore in 1806, he noted that the 'fir tribe' rather 'preponderates too much' and suggested that the 'judicious application of the axe' should be applied to the demesne's extensive plantations.[39] Colt Hoare had a particular dislike for the spikes of emergent crowns of conifers, so much so indeed, that in 1792 he had controversially removed the firs from the Fir Walk at Stourhead.[40]

At Tollymore Colt Hoare may have picked on the wrong species, for Clanbrassill had also extensively planted *Rhododendron ponticum* from around 1794, until then considered a specimen shrub, to brighten up the sombre woods. These are among the earliest known plantings of *R. ponticum* in Ireland.[41] Little did he know that they would overrun the woods and banks of the river so quickly, for already by the 1840s they had 'scattered through the woods', many attaining large sizes, having been found 'fully as hardy as the common laurel'.[42]

In addition to larch and Scotch pine plantations, Clanbrassill added many new species of trees and shrubs to the four hectare pleasure grounds, which he created in the area to the west of the house. These grounds, which are shown on Scalé's 1777 map, included two summer-houses, both of which have disappeared; one of them, which was close to the walled garden, lasted until the 1950s and had a tiled floor depicting a classical scene of a fox attacking chickens. The new plantings included many of the new introductions that were arriving at this time from eastern North America as well as from Europe, China and Chile.[43]

One tree very closely associated with Tollymore, is the variety of dwarf spruce, *Picea abies* 'Clanbrassiliana'. According to Loudon writing in 1844, it was first discovered by Clanbrassill when out hunting in what had been Sir Arthur Rawdon's estate at Moira in County Down.[44] It is a compact, very slow-growing bushy tree which lives to a great age. Having brought the original tree to Tollymore, Clanbrassill subsequently introduced it to the English market. What is reputed to be the original tree still survives at Tollymore, although it nearly came to grief during the 1940s when hit by a military jeep. In 1955 it was measured as being 5.08 metres tall.[45] The 'Clanbrassiliana' is not a particularly remarkable tree and is of more interest on account of its rarity and association with Tollymore.[46]

*Picea abies* 'Clanbrassiliana'

The Earl of Clanbrassill, along with the Earl of Charlemont and the Earl of Moira, was one of the founding members of the Royal Irish Academy. The academy was set up to promote 'the study of science, polite literature and antiquities'. He was also a member of the Society of Dilettanti along with his friend the Marquess of Monthermer.[47] Both of them were elected president on different occasions. The main interest of the Society was the architectural and archaeological remains of Italy and other Mediterranean countries. It financed expeditions and laid the foundations for the serious and systematic study of classical antiquities, at the same time adding to the British Museum's treasures.

Decoration on a carved plinth in the present car park, a relic of the Earl of Clanbrassill's art collection

At one point Clanbrassill was entrusted with the Society's antiquities which he kept at his London residence. Among Clanbrassill's art collection were various sculptures and artefacts, the last item of which to remain at Tollymore is the now much-weathered early plinth at present in the car park. On election to the Society a member generally had his portrait painted by the Society's nominated artist, unless he paid what became known as 'face money' amounting to one guinea per annum. Sir Joshua Reynolds was the Society's painter at that time, but Clanbrassill preferred to be drawn by Jean-Etienne Liotard who visited England in the early 1770s (see page 48).[48] In his portrait, Clanbrassill is wearing a splendid red velvet coat. Mrs Delany, who had accompanied him on the long and often unpleasant journey over to England, wrote that,

> *Lord Clanbrassill was mighty interesting on board ship in his red velvet gown with fur, and he wanted to play at the Ace of Diamonds and to strip himself in order to give his garment to my sister. He was sick with*

*the utmost dignity, and assured us all very many times that he never was sick as other people were.*[49]

To his friends Clanbrassill was a personable host. When Sir James Caldwell, renowned for his Epicurean tastes, stayed with Clanbrassill, his host apologised for not providing sufficient fruit, 'after what he had heard of Castle Caldwell and its desserts'. But apart from finding the fruit below his own standards, Sir James enjoyed his visit to Tollymore:

*The living here is very elegant, much in the French way, few things substantial. It is the fashion to have the desert laid on the table after the second course without the cloth being taken away, and the bottles and glasses set down again. The dessert is made out of creams, conserves and sweetmeats. No pineapples but very good melons. Their wine is excellent.*[50]

In 1783, the year when man made the first hot-air balloon ascent in Paris and William Pitt the Younger became Prime Minister, George III issued a warrant 'creating a Society or Brotherhood, to be called Knights of the most Illustrious Order of St Patrick'. The order was largely ceremonial, following the English and Scottish examples. The Earl of Clanbrassill was one of the original sixteen 'noble and worthy knights'. The Clanbrassill and Roden coats of arms can still be seen above the choir stalls in St Patrick's Cathedral, while the Roden standard is among those hanging in Dublin Castle today. Clanbrassill is not on record as having played a defining role in Dublin politics, often preferring his working clothes to a 'hood of sky-blue sattin, lined with a white silk'. Once more on his way to dine with Clanbrassill, Sir James Caldwell found him this time 'up to his knees in wet and dirt, with hatchet under his arm, having been all day pruning trees'.[51]

Clanbrassill followed his father as a Privy Councillor and Governor of County Louth but spent more time on his building and other pursuits at the expense of his administrative duties, a dereliction which cost him dearly in legal battles to maintain the status quo in Dundalk. But other more profound events were in the making and, as before, the epicentre was France. Three years after the Bryansford Gate had been completed, the Bastille in Paris was stormed and a National Assembly formed. The political structure in France was archaic and had not been reformed since Louis XIV's reign. The country was bankrupt, and the people denied any effective political outlet. Unlike the English and American Revolutions, which were largely domestic affairs, the French Revolution spawned yet another generation of warfare. The reverberations would be felt for more than a century, spreading out from Paris, across the Continent, and into Ireland.

Among the populace the notion had gained force that a restricted and oppressed society was not necessarily a permanent condition and that, with a concerted heave, the will of the people could be heard in a fully representative parliament. Such a straightforward idea had strong appeal to Ireland. The Society of United Irishmen was started, mainly by Presbyterians in Belfast, to reform Parliament and try and compose the sectarian differences. They sought help from France and a large fleet was dispatched to Ireland. Unprecedented storms caught the French as they tried to enter Bantry Bay, and the invasion turned into a fiasco. However, a train of events had been set in motion culminating in the 1798 Rebellion. Clanbrassill lived just long enough to learn that Lord Edward Fitzgerald, son of the Duchess of Leinster with whom the family had been on friendly terms for so long, was one of the most wanted men in Ireland, and that an uprising was imminent. His life's work must have seemed in jeopardy, but on February 6th 1798, a few weeks before the bulk of the United Irish leadership was arrested, Clanbrassill died. He was buried in St Nicholas Church, Dundalk. Sadly, there were no children to continue his line at Tollymore. Instead, his properties in Ireland and England passed to his sister who was herself a widow, her husband, the first Earl of Roden, having died the previous year.

Thus the 18th century came to a climactic end with the events in France and the Irish Rebellion, followed by the Act of Union with Great Britain two years later. But whatever the shortcomings of Irish political structures, the long period of peace that had just passed witnessed the construction of renowned architectural masterpieces and many of the great Irish demesnes. The Duke of Leinster had laid out Carton to the west of Dublin, and Powerscourt was built to Richard Castle's designs for the Wingfield family to name just two examples.[52] Tollymore, on a lesser scale but in its own distinctive style, had been created by Lord Limerick and his son the second Earl of Clanbrassill. In spite of the loss of the main house, over-planting and the neglect of the remaining buildings during the next centuries, the demesne they created is still there and discernible today.

1. Clanbrassill's control over the borough of Dundalk was especially under threat between 1782 and 1792 when his own agent, Thomas Reid, sought to capture it. See, A.P.W. Malcomson (1969) 'The struggle for control of Dundalk borough 1782-92'. *County Louth Archaeological and Historical Journal*, 17 (No.1), pp22-36.
2. The Earl of Clanbrassill was a subscriber or 'Brother'. Mr J.Ellis to Viscount Limerick (7.7.1757).
3. Emily Duchess of Leinster (a close friend of the family up to her second marriage) to Anne Hamilton (6.11.1750).
4. Grace, daughter of Thomas Foley, first Baron Foley of Kidderminster (Witley Court, Co. Worcester). The marriage took place on 21st May, 1774.
5. Lady Llanover (ed.) 1861. *The Autobiography and Correspondence of Mary Granville, Mrs Delany, 1700-1788*: Mrs Delany to Mrs Port (5.4.1774).
6. Bernard Scalé was perhaps the best topographical draftsman working in Ireland in the mid-Georgian era. He assisted his brother-in-law, John Rocque, with maps and land surveys in County Dublin (published 1756); joined in partnership with William Richards in 1762, becoming sole partner in 1774 on Richards's death. His 1760 survey of Tollymore Park is one of his earliest known works. For more on Scalé and his works see, W. G. Strickland (1913). *A Dictionary of Irish Artists*, Volume II, pp322-324 & J. Andrews, (1985). *Plantation Acres: an Historical Survey of the Irish Land Surveyor and his Maps*, pp. 162-70 and passim.
7. Between 1769 and 1774, James Hamilton, the second Earl of Clanbrassill sat as MP (Tory) for Helston in Cornwall; the seat had formerly been occupied by his brother-in-law the second Baron Godolphin of Helston. Before succeeding to his earldom, James Hamilton had sat in the Broderick seat of the borough of Midleton between 1755 and 1758.
8. The Fitzwilliam (Milton) Godolphin papers, Northamptonshire Records Office (Ref; F[M]G 862). Harriet Dowager Countess Clanbrassill to the second Baron Godolphin of Helston (11.12.1777). Baron Godolphin had married her younger sister, Barbara. He succeeded to the title on the death of his first cousin, the first Baron Godolphin (1678-1766), who had served four sovereigns with great political dexterity.
9. From Horace Walpole's celebrated 'On Modern Gardening' in *Anecdotes of Painting in England*, vol. 4 (printed 1771, but not published until 1780); the essay was published separately in 1785 as *Essay on Modern Gardening*. See also *The Works of Horace Walpole, the Earl of Orford* (1798), vol. 2, p544.
10. David Turkington's architectural survey of Tollymore describes the structural condition of the buildings, see Turkington (1999) *The Wizard of Durham and the Estate at Tollymore - The Life and Times of Thomas Wright and in Particular an Assessment of his work at Tollymore Estate County Down*. See also Gazetteer.
11. The glass panels were in the main house when it was demolished in 1952 and came in a batch from Holland. Other sections were installed in St Nicholas Church (C of I), Dundalk. Others of these panels were installed in Kilcoo Parish Church, Bryansford, in about 1812.
12. The Rev. Daniel Augustus Beaufort, Journal of a Tour through part of Ireland 1787 (Three volumes), Trinity College Dublin Library: Ms. 4028, fol. 65v. See also Canon C.C. Ellison (1975) 'Remembering Dr. Beaufort', *Quarterly Bulletin of the Irish Georgian Society*, XVIII, No. 1, p30.

13. Thomas Milton (1783-93) *Collection of Select Views from Different Seats of the Nobility and Gentry in the Kingdom of Ireland, Engraved by Thomas Milton from Original Drawings by the Best Artists*. This is an oblong quarto, containing 24 plates engraved in line after various artists. The 'Tullymore Park' plate, after John James Barralet, was published in 1787.

14. T. Mowl and B. Earnshaw (1985) *A Trumpet at a Distant Gate: the Lodge as Prelude to the Country House*; J.A.K. Dean (1994) *The Gate Lodges of Ulster*.

15. Gervase Jackson-Stops (1991). *An English Arcadia 1600-1990: Designs for Gardens and Garden Buildings in the Care of the National Trust*, pp82-3 & fig 55. Wright's pencil sketch of the gatescreen for Rothley is dated 1769; see also Eileen Harris (1971c) 'Architect of rococo landscapes: Thomas Wright. III'. *Country Life*, CL (No.3874) Sept 9th, pp.614, fig. 10; M. McCarthy (1981) 'Thomas Wright's designs for temples and related drawings for garden buildings'. *Journal of Garden History*, 1 (No.1), pp46-8. For Wright's summer-house at Nuthall Temple, see Eileen Harris (1971b) 'A flair for the grandiose', *Country Life*, CL (No.3873) Sept 2nd, pp548-50, fig. 10.

16. In 1933 the largest *Cedrus deodara* at Tollymore was measured as being 60 feet x 9 feet 10 inches (18.29 x 3.0 metres). See H.M. Fitzpatrick (1933) 'The trees of Ireland: native and introduced'. *Scientific Proceedings of the Royal Dublin Society*, 20, p613.

17. Sir Richard Colt Hoare (1807) *Journal of a Tour in Ireland A.D. 1806*, p230.

18. The date of the proposal was probably 1769. The drawings are held in Sir John Soane's Museum, London: Adam Drawings, vol. 29, Nos 80 (elevation), 81 (section) & 82 (plan). Also vol. 1, No. 217 & 218 (sketches). See also A.J. Rowan (1964) 'Georgian castles in Ireland - I'. *Quarterly Bulletin of the Irish Georgian Society*, vol. 8, No. 1 (January-March), pp3-30, especially p8; plate 6. Robert Adam designed (in 1769) a ceiling for the second Earl of Clanbrassill's house at 9 Stanhope Street, London (Sir John Soane's Museum, Adam Drawings, vol. 12, No. 27). He also designed the 'Chinese Bridge', which the Earl of Clanbrassill built on his demesne at Dundalk, since demolished (Sir John Soane's Museum, Adam Drawings, vol. 51, No 24). Elsewhere in Ireland, Adam undertook work for Hercules Rowley at Langford House, Dublin in 1765 (demolished); for the first Earl of Bective at Headfort, Co. Meath (1772-75) and for the first Baron Templemore at Castle Upton, Co. Antrim (1788-89).

19. The Fitzwilliam (Milton) Godolphin papers in the Northamptonshire Records Office (Ref: F[M] G 854). Harriet, the Dowager Countess of Clanbrassill to the second Baron Godolphin (14.10.1774). She goes on to say, 'if I was to chuse, my son should no more be in the English Parliament, it is time he should settle down as he has no turn for Publick business'.

20. Roden Papers: Lady Moira's letter to her daughter Lady Granard, May 1783.

21. The Rudhall family of Gloucester had one of the leading bell foundries in England, operating from 1684 to 1835.

22. James Howley (1993) *The Follies and Garden Buildings of Ireland*, pp38-47.

23. Roden, Earl of (ed.) *The Diaries of Lord Limerick's Grand Tour 1716-1723*. Viscount Limerick's private diary, May 1716.

24. The Marquess of Monthermer, son and heir of the Duke of Montagu, was due to inherit Boughton House in Northamptonshire. He was said to be a man of considerable taste, but died aged thirty-five. The inscription reads 'Clanbrassill to his dearest friend Monthermer'.

25. This pre-war bridge was replaced by members of the Forestry Service using local timber. It is now known as the Footstick Bridge.
26. E. Harris (1971c), *op.cit.*, p.614.
27. *Ordnance Survey Memoirs of Ireland.* A. Day and P. McWilliams (eds.) *Parishes of County Down I. 1834-6. South Down*, p44.
28. Wright retired to Byers Green in 1762. He continued to design buildings for old friends and neighbours, such as the Bishop of Durham at Auckland Castle.
29. Blanche Henrey (1975) *British Botanical and Horticultural Literature Before 1800*, vol. II, p645. John, the fourth Duke of Atholl (1755-1830) succeeded to his father's estates in 1774.
30. During his visit to Dunkeld, the Earl of Clanbrassill may well also have seen the hermitage, known as 'Ossian's Hall', built by the third Duke of Atholl (in 1758 and modified 1783) overlooking the dramatic falls on the Braan river.
31. John Claudius Loudon (1844) *Arboretum et Fruticetum Britannicum*, I, p.108.
32. Roden Papers: Almanac for 1789 (Dorse Note). See also L. Proudfoot (1992) 'Landscaped demesnes in pre-famine Ireland: a regional case study', in A. Verhoeve and A. J. Vervloet (eds). *The Transformation of the European Rural Landscape: Methodological Issues and Agrarian Change 1770-1914*, pp230-237.
33. Loudon (1844) *op.cit.*, vol. I, p110.
34. Roden Papers. Almanac for 1789 (Dorse Note).
35. Loudon (1844) *op.cit.*, p110, mentions that one silver fir planted at Tollymore in the early 1780s had by 1844 grown to '84 ft. high; the diameter at 1 ft. from the ground, 5ft. 2in; at 10 ft., 4ft ; and at 24 ft., 3ft. 3in; it is beautiful and evenly clothed with branches, the lower tiers of which are pendent to the ground and the circumference of the space which they cover is 160ft'.
36. B. Henrey (1975) *op.cit.*, p574, argues convincingly that the author of this treatise was James Fortescue (1725-1782) of Ravensdale Park. He was the younger brother of the Earl of Clermont. It was later published as a section in William Boutcher's book on the cultivation of trees *A Treatise on Forest-trees* (Dublin, 1786).
37. Tollymore larch was much in demand by boatbuilders. The author's gaff-rigged Galway Hooker is built from Tollymore larch.
38. Loudon (1844) *op.cit.*, vol. I, p110.
39. Colt Hoare (1806) *op.cit.*, p230. Sir Richard Colt Hoare (1758-1838) inherited Stourhead in 1783, where he added many new species of trees and shrubs.
40. K. Woodbridge (1982) *The Stourhead Landscape*, p34; M. Lear (1987) The Woody Plant Catalogue – a Basis for Garden Management and Plant Conservation. MSc Thesis, University of Aberdeen, p410. The tree species at the centre of this controversial move at Stourhead has been the subject of some speculation. Lear (1987) *op.cit.*, considers them to be Weymouth Pine (*Pinus strobus*), an east North American species, which initially showed promise as a large scale forestry species. Colt Hoare probably encountered these trees at Tollymore.
41. The earliest *R. ponticum* planted in Ireland was probably at Oriel Temple, Co. Louth in 1778; see P. Bowe and K. Lamb (1995) *A History of Gardening in Ireland*, Glasnevin, p55. In Great Britain *R. ponticum* was introduced to Kew from the Botanic Garden in Gibraltar in 1763

and was first established in Hampshire in 1763, see I. Rotherham (2002) 'The ecology and history of *R. ponticum*' in G Argent & M McFarlane (eds) *Rhododendrons in Horticulture and Science*, p234. However, it was not until the 1770s and 1780s that it was sent out commercially from Loddiges of Hackney; see W.J. Bean (1976) *Trees and Shrubs*, vol. III, p742; D. Solman (1995) *Loddiges of Hackney*, p24.

42. Loudon (1844) *op.cit.*, vol. I, p110. Loudon also remarked that one of the *R. ponticum* at Tollymore 'at 50 years of age' was '10 ft. high, and covers, with its unbroken mass of foliage, a space the circumference of which is 90 ft'.

43. There is no list of the exotic trees planted at Tollymore by the second Earl of Clanbrassill. However, among those he planted were the Tulip tree, Silver Fir, Maritime Pine and the Cork Oak.

44. Loudon (1844) *op.cit.*, vol. IV, p2294-2295. Sir Arthur Rawdon (1662-1695) created a very important garden at Moira, substantial relics of which still remained in the later 18th century when the property was owned by his descendant, John Rawdon (1720-93), who was created Earl of Moira in 1762. Loudon, in reporting the story of the discovery of the tree, added that 'It appears to us very doubtful whether such a stunted variety as this was ever found in a bed of seedlings: we think it much more probable that it is a continuation by cuttings of one of those bird-nest-like monstrosities that are occasionally found on all trees'.

45. In 1911 the tree was recorded as being 3 metres high (10 feet); in 1920 it was 3.48 metres high (11 feet 5 inches) and in 1955 it was 5.08 metres high (16 feet 8 inches), while the circumference of its crown was 11.80 metres (38 feet 9 inches). *Gardening Illustrated*, 73 (February 1956), p40; Forest Service (1964), *Tollymore Forest Park*, p21. Being so slow to grow, this variety is difficult to date, but it was said to be 200 years old in the 1955 guidebook. However, Loudon (Appendix 5) says several were planted, so the tree hit by the WWII jeep may have been planted at any time between 1750 and c.1820.

46. *Picea abies* 'Clanbrassiliana' grow less than 6cm a year. They rarely exceed a height of 2m and are usually only between 0.60m to 1m. It is possible that the Tollymore tree may be starting to revert. The plant is sterile. However, it is recorded as growing wild in Central Germany and Sweden. Good specimens, which originated from the Tollymore tree, are at Abbeyleix and Castlewellan. It was well known by the beginning of the 1800s; John Templeton obtained a young plant from Tollymore in August 1804. The related tree *Picea abies* 'Clanbrassiliana Stricta' was discovered, according to J.C. Loudon, in the park at Florence Court, Co. Fermanagh in 1834, see Loudon (1844) *op.cit.*, vol. IV, p2295; also Charles Nelson (1984) *An Irish Flower Garden*, pp51-52.

47. Lionel Cust (1898) *History of the Society of Dilettanti* (ed.) Sidney Colvin.

48. The pastel portrait of the Earl of Clanbrassill, and another of his wife, both dated 1774, are now in a private collection in Geneva. Both pictures are reproduced in Brian De Breffny (1987) 'Liotard's Irish paintings'. *Irish Arts Review*, 4, No. 2 (Summer) p35.

49. Lady Llanover (ed.) 1861. *The Autobiography and Correspondence of Mary Granville, Mrs Delany, 1700-1788*: Mrs Delany to her friend Emily Duchess of Leinster, 30.1.1771. In addition to composing well-received poetry, she was prone to writing critical opinions of others.

50. T.W.Bagshawe, *The Bagshawes of Ford* as quoted in Valerie Pakenham (2000) *The Big House in Ireland*, p28.
51. V. Pakenham (2000) *op.cit.*, p28.
52. Two generations of Roden daughters married into the Wingfield family.

Foley's bridge with ladies posing in the foreground, c.1880.

CHAPTER 5

# The Roden Era

When the Union Jack, incorporating the Cross of St Patrick, was flown for the first time on New Year's Day 1801 following the Act of Union, it aroused little interest among the people of Ulster. Hunger, harvest failure and the devastation of war were uppermost in their minds. The flaws in Henry Grattan's Parliament had been rudely exposed by the 1798 Rebellion and French incursions. In a major emergency, Ireland still depended on England for military and financial support. When the earlier confidence that had been evident in the Volunteer movement and among the reformers evaporated, the Act of Union became an inevitability. At the time of the Rebellion, and indeed afterwards, fear stalked the land. The revelations that still trickled in from France haunted the Establishment. For the victors there was the fear for their long-term security. For the defeated it was a fear of what the future held for them, their families and their cause. It was a fear that bred arrogance and intolerance. The admirable theories of the United Irishmen to bring all Irish factions together had metamorphosed into a minority power group who were driven to look after their own interests wherever and whenever possible. The same fear would induce them to overreact in peace as some had done in war under the ever-present threat of the Roman Catholic majority. The French Revolution may have triggered long-needed reform in its own country, but the tumultuous events in France would affect the rest of Europe for many years to come.

The year 1798 was, therefore, not the most propitious period for an elderly widow to take over the reins of the Clanbrassill estates; but Anne Countess of Roden, the Earl of Clanbrassill's sister and heir, rose to the occasion, as her namesake and grandmother, Anne Hamilton, had done a hundred years previously. 'Now are my duties increased to a serious degree; may I be enabled to perform them as faithfully in the sight of God as I earnestly and sincerely desire to do it,' she wrote in her diary, going on to say that 'the possession of a

Half-length portrait of Robert Jocelyn, first Earl of Roden by Hugh Douglas Hamilton, dated 1797

large fortune is an alarming charge'. She was now responsible for the Clanbrassill properties in England, Dublin, Dundalk, Galway, Meath, Tipperary and Down, including Tollymore. Her husband, Robert Jocelyn, the first Earl of Roden, had died only in 1797, and the two portfolios would be combined on her own death four years later when her son, the second Earl of Roden, added her inheritance to his own.[1]

But the assessment of her new 'large fortune' would have to take second place to the family's safety. Writing in her diary she recorded:

> Wednesday 23rd May 1798. *Louisa, the Hutchinsons, and I came to Tollymore Park. This day began with dreadful scenes in and about Dublin which, as we came farther north, we were ignorant of for two days: dreadful indeed they are, but mercy has attended me and supported me under the dreadful apprehension from reports yesterday that this shocking rebellion had broke out at Belfast and Drogheda, so that all I loved on all*

*sides were in danger, except the single one who was with me; and even we appeared from that report to be between two fires, which would soon destroy us. June 7th. In the evening, Gray* [her agent] *asked me if I should not like to have some troops, that were at Bryansford, guard this house. I was rather startled at the question as I apprehended he might have heard some alarming account; and he said No, and I refused the guard. In less than a hour after, I received an express from Harriot to inform me that there was a rising in Larne which they hoped would soon be got under; but urging me most eagerly to set out immediately for Belfast, for which purposes she had sent her horses to meet me at Saintfield, and also an order from General Nugent that six dragoons that were stationed at Bryansford should escort me. This account was most alarming. We waited for break of day, and set out in our chaise and Miss Hutchinson's chaise. Louisa recollected that Captain Wolseley was in the neighbourhood, and wrote to ask him to accompany us, which he most kindly complied with; and we found him upon our road to Clough. We got with perfect safety to Belfast.*[2]

Two days later Anne gathered up her family and took ship to Scotland, returning to Tollymore later in September after the worst of the Rebellion was over.

Anne now endeavoured to bring some order to her late brother's estate. First and foremost she discovered that it was heavily encumbered with debt, which the Earl of Clanbrassill had done little to reduce or even service. With a war-ravaged countryside and poor harvests, the return from rents was low and the market for property depressed. The debt chargeable to Tollymore on the Earl of Clanbrassill's death was £4,392 of which £1,800 was interest. Set against this was a theoretical annual income of £1,200 from which the general running costs and wages had to be met. But settle she did. Among the accounts was one outstanding for building work done at Tollymore. 'To paid Dickson, the mason, half year's salary ending May 1798 as per agreement with Lord Clanbrassill - £37.5s.8p.'[3]

Not withstanding the aftermath of war and the financial reorganization of the estates, there was still work to be completed. The countess's younger son, John Jocelyn, wrote to his mother about alterations being carried out to the farm and garden buildings: 'You have such a pretty taste for building that I am sure you will have it well executed'.[4] He may have been trying to flatter his mother, but she had, after all, been tutored by Thomas Wright. The following year her steward at Tollymore, Charles Moore, sent her a letter about estate matters and went on

Half-length portrait of Robert Jocelyn, second Earl of Roden, dated 1817

to say: 'I visited your Ladyship's new road last week. It is very well executed and the bridge goes on well'.[5] Unfortunately, there is no record of which bridge he was referring to.

A portrait of Anne Dowager Countess of Roden, painted in old age, shows her as a kind and competent-looking woman.[6] Had she lived longer, she might have brought even greater order to the Clanbrassill estates. On her death in 1802, Tollymore passed to her son Robert, the second Earl of Roden.[7]

In 1768, Anne's husband, the first earl, had built Brockley Park in County Leix, for his family to the design of the Sardinian architect, Davis Ducart.[8] Beside his other estates in Ireland, the second earl also inherited the Hyde Hall properties in East Anglia along with the English baronetcy.[9] The beginning of the new century thus saw the very apogee of the combined land ownership and fine art collections, so much so that the second earl must have been faced with some interesting decisions as to where to set down his roots, if at all. Fortunately for future generations he chose Tollymore as his principal residence, preferring the mountainous landscape to the flatter plains of Leix or his other home in England.

The second earl soon started to make changes to the demesne. His sister, Lady Caroline Jocelyn, wrote a rather gloomy letter to her nephew Robert, afterwards the third earl. 'We came [to Dundalk] by way of Tollymore which looked very cold and bleak, however your father is going on there with many improvements'.[10] Writing in 1805 to the earl's eldest son, Viscount Jocelyn, the family's Irish agent, John Straton, reported:

> *your father has greatly improved Tollymore, finished the back entrance elegantly, built a new piggery and is now making a fence so as to move the deer near the Barbican Gate that they may be seen from the house. All the furze and weeds and underwood are stubbed up and Pepys Cottage is to be made a beautiful object and fitted up for dining in. By next summer the whole face of the Park will wear a different appearance.*

He then went on to observe: 'I am truly glad he has found some situation to allow him to stay in Ireland, and as Lady Roden seems quite fond of it, I dare say he will not change for Hyde Hall'.[11]

The small deer park that was created in 1805 covered some 26 hectares and occupied the open parkland area between the Barbican Gate and the entrance front of the house.[12] The main avenue passed through the centre of this open park meadow, while the enclosing fence ran alongside or perhaps inside the surrounding woodland belts and screens. The creation of this park reflected the increasing fashion for deer parks to be seen as ornamental features and not just as venison farms and hunting areas. Consequently, the nineteenth century saw a number of small, carefully designed deer parks being created in demesnes near to the house so that the deer could be admired from the windows.[13]

One of the additions to the property was a new glasshouse in the kitchen gardens to the north of the house. In the schedule of the second earl's debts, which were many, there is an item for work there, 'Amount of bill furnished for greenhouse to 1st May 1811 - £223.2s.4d'. At this time glasshouses were still comparatively rare in Ireland and were only confined to homes of the very rich. It was not until the repeal of the glass tax in 1845 and the dramatic improvements in the technology of glass and cast-iron manufacture around that time, that the widespread production of glasshouses became possible. The glasshouse built at Tollymore in 1811 would probably have had small panes, slotted into closely spaced glazing bars.[14] It is not certain where this building was located, but it

Map by Stephen Gribbin of the small deer park at Tollymore, surveyed February 1805. The main drive from the Barbican Gate to the house passes through the centre of this park

possibly formed part of a substantial wooden glasshouse in the upper part of the walled garden, where the present car park is now. From an early photograph of this building, we know that it comprised a large central gable-ended conservatory of mid 19th-century appearance, flanked by lean-to glasshouse ranges, maybe of earlier date.

The family history paints a somewhat flattering picture of the second earl, having been written at a time when many of his near family were still alive. 'He was a very deservedly popular Nobleman, of an amiable disposition and pleasing manners'.[15] His popularity would have been confined to the Establishment as he rushed headlong to its defence at the outset of the 1798 Rebellion. Like other able-bodied men of his day, he raised his own regiment, the First Fencible Dragoons. It became known as the Roden Foxhunters, because the enlisting

The main glasshouse in the upper section of the walled garden, circa 1865. The central conservatory is flanked by lean-to ranges which would have contained the vinery and peach houses. In the background lies the Clanbrassill Barn

sergeants promised new recruits a day's hunting each week. Hunting or otherwise, they played a minor, albeit notorious, part in the Rebellion and also saw action when the French landed at Killala Bay in County Mayo to support an uprising which by that time had collapsed.[16]

Buoyed up by his military experiences, the second earl enjoyed the companionship of the Prince of Wales and the extravagant lifestyle of the Regency period. He maintained his interests in Ireland mainly through hunting and racing, being a founder member of the Irish Turf Club. He also followed his forebears as Governor of County Louth, as Auditor-General for Ireland and a Knight of St Patrick. If his mother had tried to bring order to the estates, she failed to impress the need for fiscal propriety on her son. The Earl of Clanbrassill's homes in England were sold off, to be followed soon afterwards by other properties in Ireland.[17]

This took place when Irish agriculture was going through one of its few golden periods of the 19th century, thanks to Napoleon Bonaparte. The war with France, which had been fought largely at sea by Horatio Nelson and financed at a distance by England, drew to a close with the Treaty of Amiens in 1802, the year the second earl inherited Tollymore. The war then burst into life again in 1803 and was to continue until Napoleon's final defeat and banishment to St Helena twelve years later. To supply the army's wartime demands, the prices of most commodities soared, to the benefit of Ireland's farmers and industry.[18] However, so did taxation. After the Act of Union, the Irish representation at Westminster became an ineffectual minority. Ireland was ruled in a cynical fashion, and events elsewhere took precedence over the interests of what the English considered an alien, troublesome neighbour. Moreover, Ireland soon realized that it had to raise money not only to finance the country, but to pay its share of the Imperial expenses along with the rest of the Union. England's promises of greater commercial advantage and Catholic emancipation had been proved worthless, as many had foretold. Power was centred in London, and all those seeking influence and preferment in a monolithic, social structure had to spend the greater part of their time in England. During the economic depression which followed the Napoleonic Wars, Ireland's towns, cities, and countryside went into a near-terminal decline. This was perhaps inevitable, for, aside from being cut off by a difficult sea passage, Ireland had little capital, few industries; and above all, lacked its own legislature.

That the second earl was aware of his financial shortcomings is partly to his credit. On being offered the title of Marquess he declined it, pleading that his finances were not sufficient to maintain a higher rank. Nor did he have a particularly happy family life. His first wife died in middle age, in the same year he inherited Tollymore. Three of his four sons, and both daughters, all died in childhood or in their early twenties.

A fine obelisk erected 'in memory of a beloved son' stands on a small mound in line with the house and sea. It commemorates James Jocelyn, one of the second earl's sons. He joined the navy at the age of fifteen, and found himself on HMS Montague cruising off the French coast. Life at sea took a little getting used to in those days, and there were times when he regretted his decision.

> *I like the place I sleep in, they call it a Cot and it is suspended from the ceiling. Tell me how my poor mare does and I hope you do not let anyone hurt her as I always feel for dumb animals. Ask Molly Mulhall how my rabbit that I caught the day before I went away is and tell me how the hounds are. There were five men flogged about an hour ago. They were tied to the gangway and each of them got three dozen with a cat-o-nine tails and it made them very sore.*[19]

Granite obelisk commemorating James Jocelyn, one of the second Earl of Roden's sons, who died in 1812

The next year saw his ship on blockade duty off the French ports to stop the forces there joining the rest of the French fleet at Trafalgar. James's subsequent career took him to the Mediterranean, and he was soon promoted to lieutenant. But in Malta his health, which had always been suspect, deteriorated following his first bad attack of asthma. He was invalided back to Tollymore, where he appeared to recover. He even arranged for some of the old artillery pieces to be brought up from Dundalk, so that he could entertain his friends with mock battles using the White Fort as one of his defences. However, his asthma attacks returned, and he died aged twenty-three in 1812, the year Napoleon marched on Russia. The obelisk, which was once surrounded by railings, is made of ashlar granite, standing 7.60 metres high, with four inscribed slate tablets on the base. It is an elegant monument that stands out well in the landscape.

The second earl died aged sixty-four in 1820. His only surviving offspring from the first marriage, Robert Jocelyn, his eldest son, duly became the third Earl of

Robert, Viscount Jocelyn, by George Harlow R.A. 1817, when M.P. for County Louth. He became the third Earl of Roden on the death of his father in 1820

Roden and continued to maintain Tollymore as the principal family home. Prior to succeeding to the title he had sat as MP (Tory) for County Louth in the years 1806-07 and 1810-20. In 1821, he was created a peer of the United Kingdom, as Baron Clanbrassill of Hyde Hall, and this allowed him to sit in the House of Lords. At this juncture he became more focussed on religious rather than political matters. While his father had upheld the interests of the Establishment with the sword, the third earl continued the struggle with a bible. Converted to the Evangelical cause, he achieved little other than to help polarize opinions on both sides. His sister, Anne Jocelyn, was a major influence while she lived, but it is possible that his religious fervour stemmed from losing his mother and all five siblings prematurely. He, himself, records in his letters that his conversion was due to a chance attendance at a Dublin bible meeting.[20]

If an Evangelical cloud hung over Tollymore for all of the middle part of the century, the third earl did create close family bonds with his sons and daughters. With England's interests expanding rapidly across the globe after the defeat of France, Ireland's sons provided the foot soldiers, field officers, diplomats and administrators for this new empire. Whether it was opening trade links with Japan, bombarding Chinese forts during the first Opium War or, later, fighting through the Crimean winter campaigns, the third earl's sons looked back to Ireland, and particularly Tollymore, with great attachment and fondness from very far afield. Writing from the Crimea, Strange Jocelyn, afterwards the fifth Earl of Roden, said on hearing about the death of his older brother:

> *the happiest days of my life were spent at Tollymore and I shall always love the place for its thousand associations, but all that has gone now, with him whom I love more, if possible, every day.* [And again from the heights above Sevastopol] *…I feel very sad sometimes when I think of the happy days at Tollymore I used to spend with him. All my recollections are with him there – shooting etc. I cannot believe now they are all gone for ever, those happy days.*[21]

Elizabeth Bowen compared her beloved Bowen's Court in County Cork to a stage:

> *In raising a family house one is raising a theatre: one knows the existing players, guesses at their successors, but cannot tell what plays may be acted there. Time, the current of politics, debts, personalities, weather were all matters for which he* [Henry Bowen] *could not legislate. Rocking gales, limestone sweats, money embarrassments, complex affections, unhappy alienations, phases of emptiness, fashions, lonely obsessions, strictness, latitudes, children and soldiers have all left their mark on the house. A Bowen in the first place made Bowen's Court. Since then, with a rather alarming sureness, Bowen's Court has made all the succeeding Bowens.*[22]

Many Irish demesnes became their own private stages, and Tollymore was no exception. No matter what adversity, the attachments to them were binding when, in other circumstances, those responsible for looking after them might have opted for less taxing environments.

Besides creating a patriarchal, but close family, the third earl oversaw the continued development of the estate, building flax-mills along the river just outside the demesne. It was reported that he was 'farming a good deal and has a threshing machine and many other ingenious agricultural implements'.[23] In

The saw mill, circa 1865. It was built in a mountain chalet style in 1828, its date being clearly visible in the photograph on the end gable

1828, a new sawmill was built near the site of the Old Hermitage. Not only was the high-quality Tollymore larch used for boat building, general construction and implements, but when the new railways were developed along the east coast, the timber found another ready outlet. Later, it would be shipped as pit-props to the coal mines being opened up in the English Midlands. The nearby mill-ponds provided power for the sawmill, and the channels that filled the ponds stretched back to the Wooden Bridge on the main river and as far as Hore's Bridge on the Spinkwee River. To provide an even greater reservoir of water, a dam was built across a stream that flowed down to the mill-ponds, thus creating the present lake. The sawmill, which was made of local wood, was modelled on a mountain chalet. Once felled, the trees had to be manhandled or pulled by large workhorses down the steep slopes to the mill.[24]

In her *Letters from Ireland*, Charlotte Elizabeth Tonna left a contemporary description of the sawmill in operation:

The sluice gate at the Wooden Bridge

> *Lord Roden has pressed his wild river into service. Here he has erected a sawmill; and very delightful it is to see the mountain river, subdued into quiet force, steadily wending its way for a space, to work by its impetus an extensive machinery. The stream... enables a few workmen to execute the whole process of sawing, planing, turning, and finishing off every useful article, from solid timbers that support a substantial house, to the little pegs that unite the fence around it.*

Almost in the vein of a Constable painting, the author then goes on to describe the 'cottagers' coming with their carts for a valuable freight of timber and the children gathering offcuts in their pinafores.[25]

An account has been left of the launch of a three-masted sailing schooner, *The Countess of Roden*, built at Newcastle from Tollymore larch.[26] Unfortunately, the weather was far from good and the ceremony delayed as a result, so much so, that, when it came to the actual launch, the ship was stuck fast in the sand on an ebbing tide. She resisted the efforts of thousands of spectators who came forward to lend a hand and remained high and dry until the tide returned.

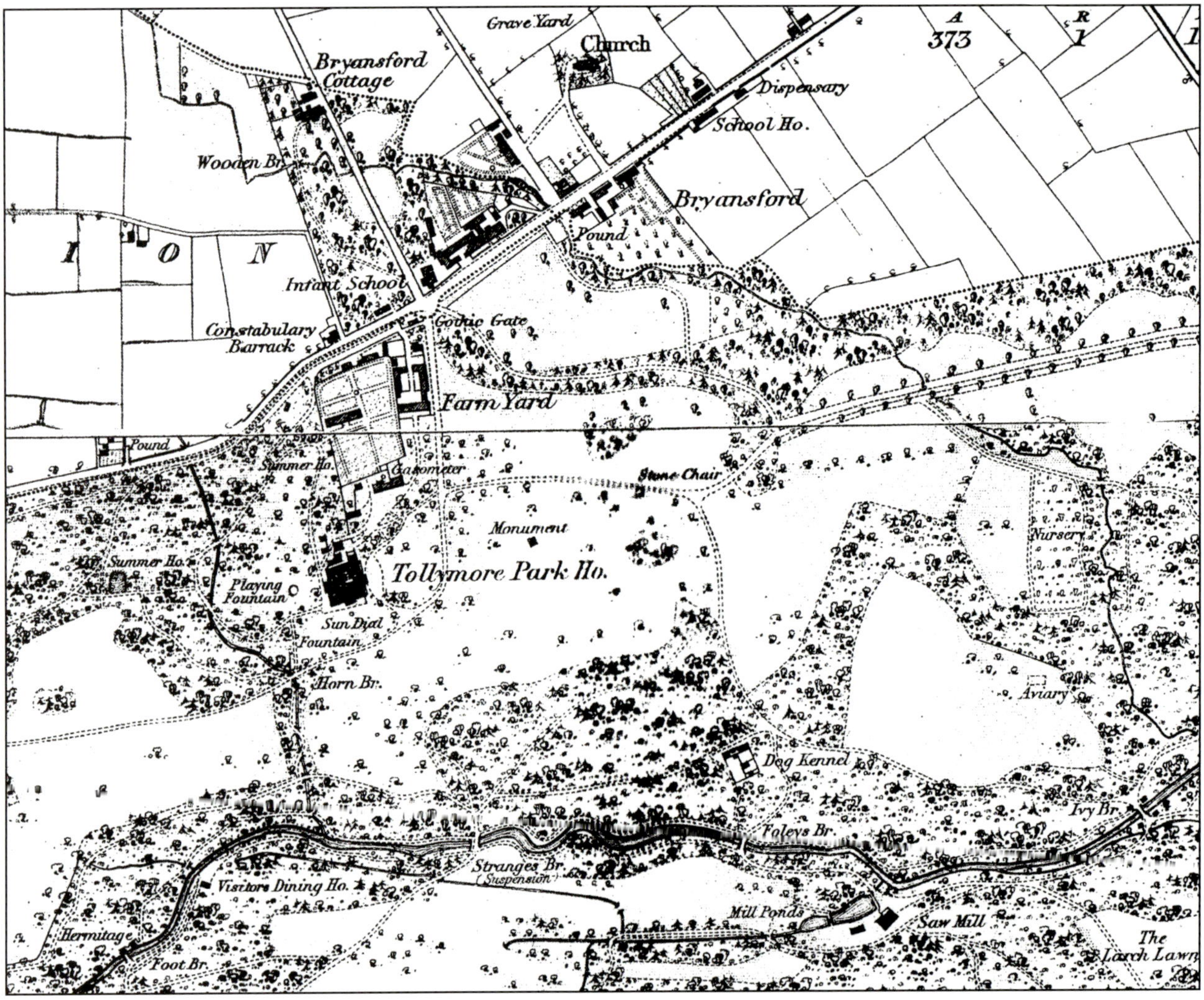

Detail of 1859 edition of Ordnance Survey sheets 43 & 49

Old Bridge, Tollymore, in winter

CHAPTER 5

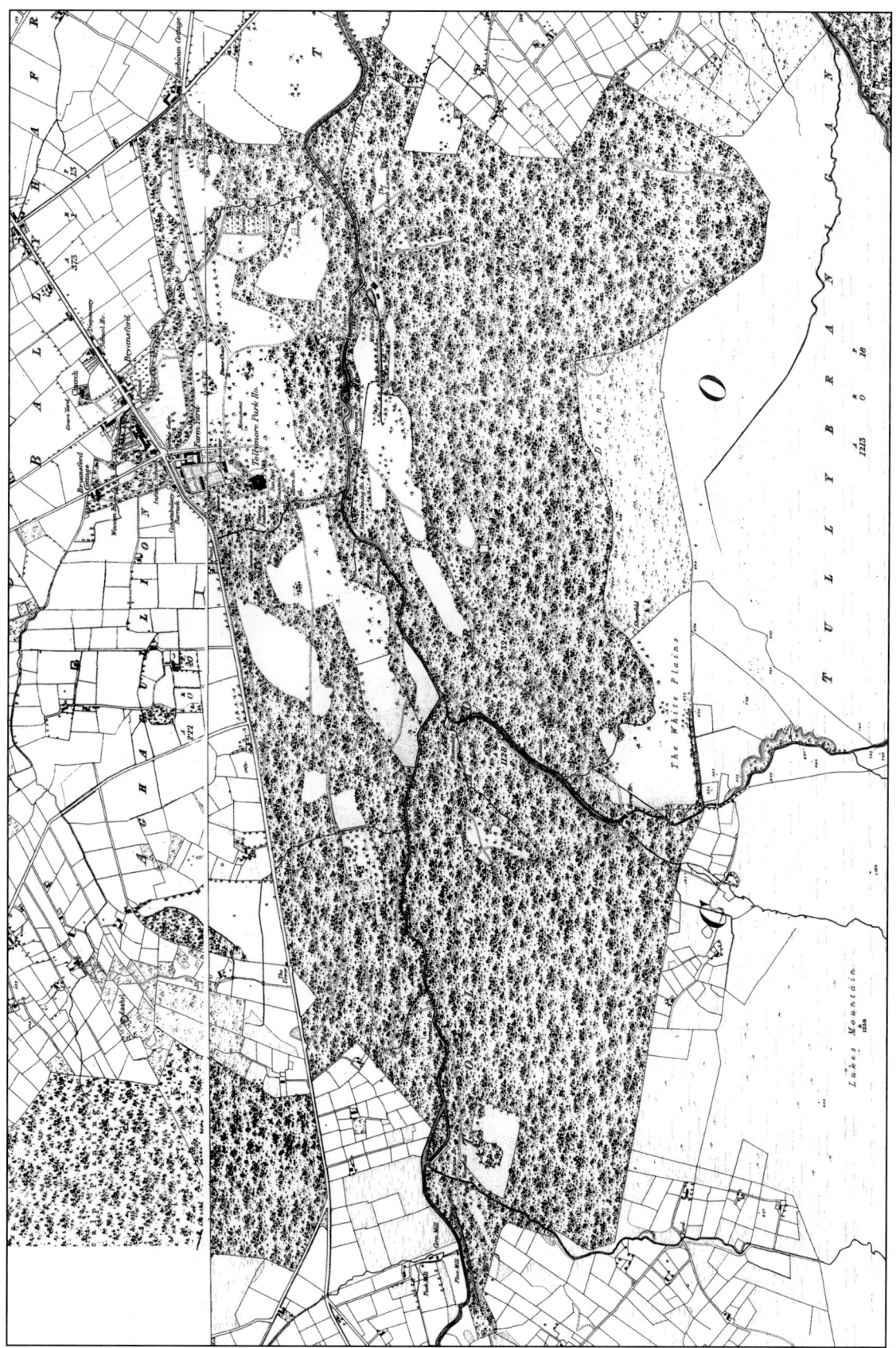

Map of Tollymore Demesne in 1859
Source: Ordnance Survey sheets 43 & 49

The Titanic's Grand Staircase made from Tollymore oak.
*Source: Titanic Historical Society*

Much later, another much more famous ship was built incorporating wood from Tollymore; this time the fine oak planted by the second Earl of Clanbrassill. She was launched more successfully in Belfast with great fanfare and much hope for the future. She was the White Star liner, *Titanic*. Thomas Andrews was the managing director and chief engineer of Harland and Wolff Ltd, the Titanic's Belfast shipbuilders. There were few aspects of the ship's construction which he did not personally supervise. The interior was fitted out to the highest standards of Edwardian luxury. The centre-piece of the first class section was the 18 metre high Grand Staircase. The panelling and carving were entirely of oak, all of it sourced from Tollymore on Andrews's express instructions, oak that had been planted a hundred and fifty years previously. Andrews, who should also have done a better job of overseeing the quality of the steel plating, was last seen standing alone in the first class apartments staring into space. Minutes later the ship split apart and disappeared below the icy waters. But not all the Earl of Clanbrassill's oak sank 3000 metres to the seabed. Torn asunder by the pressure and the collapse of the deck immediately above the Grand Staircase, a section of carved oak panel floated to the surface to be recovered some days later by a search vessel.[27]

Two years before the sawmill was built, the third earl had a boulder inscribed 'To the Mountain Top'. It pointed the way to the Tea House Hill, where a chalet and stables had been built for the more adventurous visitors. In 1834, the first major Ordnance Survey of County Down was completed. The Survey was updated periodically and it is therefore possible to follow the new developments that took place in the demesne. More roads appear, radiating from the gamekeeper's lodge and sawmill. They were built to extract the timber from the higher slopes and the New Deer Park. In addition, two new bridges are shown since Scalé's map of 1777. One is Parnell's Bridge on the upper reaches of the main river and the other, Hore's Bridge, on the Spinkwee River.[28]

Part of a decorated four-foot long newel post belonging to the first class Grand Staircase on the Titanic. It was found floating near the scene of the disaster in April 1912 by the *Minia*, one of the ships dispatched from Halifax to search for Titanic's victims. Photograph by Joseph H. Bailey for the National Geographic Society.
*Source: National Geographic Society*

Later, sometime around 1840, a further bridge was built on Luke's River beyond Parnell's Bridge. This allowed the road into the New Deer Park to link up with the Trassey Bridge road and the mountain districts beyond the demesne. It was named Maria's Bridge after the third earl's wife, and what had been Luke's River soon had its name changed to Maria's Bridge Stream.[29]

Another change of name, albeit temporary, was Hore's Bridge to Nassau's Bridge on the Spinkwee River. Nassau Jocelyn was the youngest son of the third earl. He accompanied Lord Elgin on his diplomatic and trade mission to Japan and China in 1857.[30] In addition to his duties as a general secretary to

Inscribed boulder

Five women beside the Shimna river with the Hermitage suspension bridge in the background, circa 1870

Suspension bridge at the Hermitage, circa 1900

the Mission, he was its official photographer. His photographs of Japan, which had been closed to foreigners, were some of the first ever taken of that country. He also sent back photographs of the Yangtse River in China during the second stage of the Mission. It was the same region into which his eldest brother, Robert, had tried to force a passage seventeen years earlier.[31] Nassau and his brother Robert's wife, Lady Frances Cowper, known as Fanny Jocelyn, were part of a group of pioneering photographers in County Down. Both of them managed to take photographs of Tollymore and the mountains, some of which survive, when photographs were largely confined to studios, or had to be taken within a few minutes' quick walk of a dark room.[32]

For a while, Lord Limerick's Old Bridge became Strange's Bridge, with suspension bridges strung either side of the main structure. Another suspension bridge at the Hermitage, was shown on the 1859 edition of the Ordnance Survey map. On the River Walk between the Old Bridge and Foley's Bridge is the half section of a large boulder known as an erratic. It had been deposited at Tollymore by a glacier grinding down the valley. Having originated miles away, the erratic had been lodged in a cleft of rock where it was split by the force of ice. When the trees had been cleared around it, the third earl ordered stone-masons to inscribe

Glacial erratic on the River Walk to the east of Old Bridge. It has a biblical inscription from St John

its broken-off face with his choice of biblical instruction from St John.

In the 19th century, the Earl of Clanbrassill's gate lodges were added to, and new ones built. They were on a different scale to the Barbican and Bryansford Gate and by comparison more utilitarian structures. Gone were the days of high-arched Gothic masterpieces.

The first was an addition to the Bryansford Gate and is carefully secreted behind the wall adjacent to the main gateway. Its principal purpose was to house the gate-keeper and his family. From the early photographs (see page 9) he is shown as an ex-campaign soldier wearing a gate-keeper's uniform and his medals. His top-coat was dark blue with an orange waistcoat underneath.[33] The lodge is a single-storey, three-bay building, and the windows have lancet heads and Y tracery glass panes. The date over the doorway is inscribed 1802. It would have been built under the direction of the Earl of Clanbrassill's sister, the Dowager Countess of Roden. A new addition was also built beside the Barbican for the same purpose. Again, it was a single-storey building, with three bays and a castellated parapet. The openings all had lancet windows, and the building discreetly matched the main entrance to which it was attached by a short wall (see page 62).[34]

In 1865, a lodge was built at the east end of the demesne where the road from

The Bryansford gate lodge front façade. The date 1802 is inscribed over the doorway

Clanbrassill's Bridge followed the river towards Newcastle. It is a one-and-a-half storey gabled lodge with three bays, the centre of which has a gabled break-front. At the opposite end of the demesne, where the avenue joins the main road to Hilltown and Dundalk, the architect, John Birch, was commissioned to build a lodge which was totally out of keeping with any other work at Tollymore. It is a half-timbered Tudor-Revival building and featured in Birch's *Picturesque Lodges*: a two-storey cottage-style structure with a hipped, tiled roof.[35] The windows have an unusual tracery pattern, and on the central stone chimney is a plaque with the Roden monogram and coronet. Although it has become an integral part of Tollymore over the years, it would probably have had much the same effect on the Earl of Clanbrassill, had he lived to see it, as one of his rough sea-passages.

During the late 1830s the third earl decided to enlarge the house at Tollymore radically, transforming it from a sporting lodge into a mansion. The original rectangular block with its canted bay south front was retained, but the

The West Gate Lodge, 1876. This half-timbered Tudor-Revival building was designed by the architect John Birch

flanking single-story side wings were rebuilt as two-storey ranges in a plain late Georgian style with wide eaves and granite quoins and window surrounds. Both the returning east and west single-story wings were raised and rebuilt with nine-bay fronts, each with a three bay pedimented breakfront centre. The interior floor design, with its long corridors, followed the Earl of Clanbrassill's original scheme, while the old laundry and other outbuildings in the courtyard were retained. The main entrance remained in the east wing, where it had been previously.

The architect of the new additions has not yet been established, but it is known that the Rev. Walter Hore, who had married the third earl's cousin Harriet, was commissioned to oversee the final stage of the building works in 1841. During this period, the third earl took his wife, who was in poor health, to Italy. The 1841 works focussed on enhancing the main entrance to the house with the addition of a single storey Doric portico. At the same time the private family chapel at the back of the house was enlarged and a new floor laid. The new Doric

The east or entrance front, circa 1870. The single storey Doric portico entrance was added in 1841

The west and south fronts of the main house, circa 1870. The Venetian windows set in their rounded recesses each side of the central bow were added in the early 1840s

The west front of the main house, circa 1865-70. Continental shutters appear never to have been added to this side of the building

portico undoubtedly gave the house an aspect of grandeur; it had steps on either side of a granite ashlar perron, leading to a large classical door with a projecting cornice, supported by consoles. Adding further to the building's new splendour was a pair of Venetian windows set within elaborate arched recesses each side of the canted bow of the original 18th-century block. Curiously, louvred external shutters were added to all the windows on the entrance front as well as to those on the first floor of the south front; these gave the house a rather continental air, but were later removed in 1878-9.

Bad weather held up the work in 1841, but it allowed Hore to build an ice-house nearby.[36] In those days ice had to be cut when the lakes near Castlewellan froze over. It was then carted the five kilometres to Tollymore and packed with a thick insulation of straw. A well-prepared ice-house would last a family through most of the summer months, but involved much hard work in cold conditions. The carter bringing the ice from Castlewellan often had to ride on the back of the horses to avoid being frozen.

Relief work during the famine years saw more construction work at Tollymore.

Prior to the Great Famine of 1845-51, there had been periodic failures of the potato crop which foreshadowed what lay in store. Until a French farmer unintentionally sprayed his potatoes with chemicals used to protect his adjacent vines, no antidote could be found to the new, microscopic fungus, *Phytophthora infestans*. It could strike within hours, leaving in its path a stinking wasteland and families facing starvation. The people of Ulster had tended to augment their diet with meal and, as a result, were not so destitute as other districts in the south and west of the country, but this was little consolation. Sir Robert Peel, the British Prime Minister, tried to alleviate the problem by repealing the Corn Laws, thereby deflating the artificial market and allowing the importation of cheaper grain. When English land-owning interests rounded on him, it brought his political career to an end and greatly worsened the situation in Ireland. The new Government turned to the civil servant, Sir Charles Trevelyan, who reduced the distribution of subsidized food in favour of more public work. The starving had to work for their food but, by that time, famine and disease were so serious that no amount of harbours and highways would ameliorate the disaster. At Tollymore, food was provided for families in distress, and work found where possible for the able-bodied. Up to one hundred jobs were available in the forests, house and gardens. But the only additional work that could be commissioned at the family's expense was drainage and more walls around the demesne or in the mountains. The six-man hand-barrows, which appeared at this time, were capable of carrying half a ton of stone each - if the men were fit and well enough for the task.[37]

If the Great Famine was responsible for walling in many Irish demesnes, it finally changed attitudes towards rule from Westminster and land tenure. Both would be reformed in time, but only after relentless pressure against entrenched interests.

While the famine still raged across the country and Belfast was in the grips of a cholera epidemic, members of the local Orange Lodge announced in 1849 that they would march from Rathfriland, through the Annesley Estate at Castlewellan and on to Tollymore. The procession, armed and accompanied by bands, made the long march to Tollymore, where they were addressed by, among others, the third earl who called for calm and reasonable behaviour. The procession then re-formed and, against earlier official advice, took the same route home. Firing broke out as the Orangemen passed through Dolly's Brae outside Castlewellan. A number of Catholics were killed, homes were burnt and the marching song, *Dolly's Brae*, which raps out how they walked 'all round Lord Roden's Park', entered the pantheon of sectarian balladry.[38]

On another, earlier occasion in 1836 an assault was planned on Tollymore. It would not be the last. In his *Notes on a Short Tour through the Midland Counties of Ireland*, Baptist Noel recorded:

> *a large and tumultuous body…assembled in the neighbourhood and marched on [Lord Roden's] gate, while he was in England, threatening to level the house with the ground. There they were met by about twenty-five of his servants, who, with arms presented, declared that the rioters should only pass to that house over their dead bodies. During this parley, which already staggered the invaders, the menace of a bloody vengeance, should they dare to touch a stone of the house, was sent to them by a large body of Orangemen, who were hastily assembling. The message completed their dismay. The enterprise was too hazardous, and the place was saved. But since that time, as a precaution, forty muskets, in perfect order, have been ranged in the hall at Tollymore, with the ancient armour, as if to show that modern civilisation has only improved the weapons of war, but not rendered them unnecessary. Notwithstanding this incident, Lord Roden has lived in fearless and friendly intercourse with his neighbours.*[39]

The third earl, apart from his proselytising, was considered a fair and progressive landlord. The houses on the estate were built according to pre-arranged plans. To help the poorer tenants the third earl provided Welsh slate, or advanced the price of the slate for one year, as he considered slate more economical than thatch in the long term. He also introduced an additional facility known as the Bryansford Loan Fund, to which he subscribed £2,500. If, before he had sold his crops, a tenant wanted money for seed, fertiliser, or indeed to pay his rent, he could draw on the fund free of interest. All parties benefited and no one is known to have defaulted. In some years the total Fund revolved more than three times over.

The continuous waves of cholera that spread across Europe in the mid-19th century did not spare the Roden family. In 1854, Viscount Robert Jocelyn, the third earl's eldest son and heir, was quartered at the Tower of London with his regiment. He had survived the privations of the China campaign and became an active member of Parliament on his return to London.[40] Feeling unwell, he tried to make his way home from the Tower, but succumbed en route, becoming just another of the 20,000 people to die in England that year alone from *Pestilential Cholera*.[41]

The countryside, over which Robert and his brother, Strange, used to shoot and fish together when they were younger offered a variety of sport. The fortnightly

Robert, the third Earl of Roden, pointing to a petition. Engraving by Thomas Lupton based on a portrait by F. R. Say, R.A, dated 1839

return for the house and farm dated October 1840, shows twenty-one salmon caught in the river, and the Tollymore game book recorded over a hundred brace of woodcock to the brothers' guns. The steep plantations were not ideal habitats for game, even though blackcock had been introduced in 1834. The golden eagles soaring over the Mournes would have been delighted, but a few years later they would disappear. The same fate befell the buzzard in the 1870s, all as a result of the use of strychnine to control vermin.[42] Among the unusual birds recorded at Tollymore were the first breeding pair of crossbills in 1836.

The period between the Great Famine and the 1870s saw a steady rise in agricultural prices, helped this time by the Crimean War. Flax gave a high cash crop to small farmers, and those who had not perished or emigrated experienced a relatively prosperous period in their lives. Rents could be paid, and the third earl looked around for further ideas to improve his property during what would be the final years of his tenure. The 1859 edition of the Ordnance Survey six-inch map shows a gasometer to the rear of the main house. Gas was first successfully

The west front of the main house, circa 1890. This front remained largely unaltered after the 1878 fire. In the foreground lies a fountain and mounded flower beds

used to illuminate a house in Durham in 1780.⁴³ Sir Walter Scott tried it, but found it was odorous and required a lot of coal to provide any worthwhile light. The system had been refined by the time it was installed at Tollymore, but it still used up vast quantities of bituminous coal. The house only turned over to electricity in 1927.

When the third Earl of Roden died in 1870, he was succeeded by his grandson Robert, owing to the death of his eldest son from cholera in 1854. But the young fourth earl did not enjoy the best of health; suffering from tuberculosis, he had to spend much of his time in the South of France. One evening in January 1878, while the earl was away, a tenant farmer, Michael Joyce, decided to take a shortcut through the demesne after work. To his surprise he noticed flames shooting from the centre of the house and rushed on to Bryansford to raise the alarm, frantically ringing the church bell to summon help. The proprietors of the Roden Arms, police, farm workers and even the Coast Guards, who had seen the flames from Newcastle, hurried to the scene. A runner was dispatched to Annesborough, outside Castlewellan, to call the fire engine from Murland's Works, and it arrived a few hours later. In the meantime, ladders were placed against the sides of the burning building and buckets passed up to the men on the roof in an attempt to control the flames. Down below, the housekeeper and assorted helpers managed,

The south and east fronts of the main house, circa 1910. This picture shows James Rawson Carroll's centre block, remodelled in a French château manner after the fire of 1878.
*Source: Folk and Transport Museum, W. A. Green Collection, 564*

View down a corridor on the ground floor looking into the main staircase, circa 1880

Family group standing on the main staircase, circa 1880. On the left can be seen the regimental standards of the First Fencible Dragoons, later known as the 'Roden Foxhunters'

with considerable courage, to save the fine art collection. They also managed to prevent the fire spreading to the adjoining wings, but the main section of the house was extensively damaged.[44]

The burnt 18th-century block of the house was rebuilt later in 1878 under the direction of the architect James Rawson Carroll of Dublin.[45] He added high mansard roofs to the central block, crowned by decorative ironwork and enlivened with tall chimneystacks and segmental headed dormers. The French château manner he used was very popular at the time, though its use at Tollymore was perhaps incongruous, besides making the building appear lop-sided when viewed from the entrance front.[46] Carroll also added two bands of string coursing between the ground and first floor windows on the east and south fronts and installed segmental pediments over the first floor windows of the canted bow. The next summer, a new water system was installed, using 4-inch cast-iron pipes joined with 'a mixture of white and red lead', and stretching 4,000 yards across to the Spinkwee River at the cost of 3s.9d. per yard.

The oval drawing room, circa 1880

The following year, in January 1880, the fourth Earl of Roden died in France aged thirty-four, and Tollymore passed to his uncle, John Strange Jocelyn, the veteran of the Crimea. After the loss of his brother, Strange had had misgivings about returning to the scene of their happy childhood, but he rose to the occasion and did all he could to manage the Roden estates.

These were trying times for Irish landlords. Michael Davitt had formed the Land League in 1879 to try and give tenants better security of tenure and a reduction in rents, which were as high and sometimes higher than corresponding rents in England. The more extreme elements in the movement just wanted an end to all landlordism. To give greater political impetus to the Land League, Davitt chose Charles Stewart Parnell, himself a Protestant and large landowner, as its President. Parnell's great grandfather, Sir John Parnell, had been an active Volunteer who vehemently opposed the Act of Union. Parnell's American grandfather on his mother's side had defeated the English at sea in 1812. Not surprisingly, his ambition was to sever, by political means, all links with England

The library in 1877. Watercolour by Lady Mary Ponsonby

bar the link with the crown. In an attempt to broaden the movement's appeal and placate Ulster, he proclaimed: 'Protestants will form a most valuable element in Irish legislature...exercising a moderating influence in making laws. We want all creeds and classes in Ireland'. When the League was outlawed and then effectively dismantled by Parnell in 1882, many estate owners breathed a sigh of relief - but not for long. After the election of 1885, Gladstone found that his Liberal Party depended on the support of the Irish Nationalists to stay in power. He attempted to bring in a Home Rule Bill, and although he used all his remarkable powers of oratory, the Bill was defeated. There would be other attempts to bring in Home Rule but, for some, the stage was gradually being set for future change by force of arms.

However, a series of bills, starting in 1885 with the Purchase of Land Act (the Ashbourne Act), proved far easier to pass through Parliament. The legislation entitled a tenant to become the owner of the land he farmed, bought out by the State advancing mortgages to the tenant, who ended up paying an interest figure often lower than his existing rent. Further Land Acts gradually incorporated the principle of compulsory purchase and then an added monetary inducement should the landlord sell his entire estate, bar his private demesne, en masse. While the national question had not been resolved, the greater part of Ireland changed ownership quietly and peacefully.

Strange, the fifth Earl of Roden, was already fifty-seven when he returned to Tollymore and he had no male heir.[47] He died in 1897, the year Germany decided to embark on a major expansion of its Navy, and England was dragged slowly but surely into a very expensive war with the Boers of South Africa.

Not only did the family have to pay the new death duties for the first time, they had to find an heir to the estates and the title. Nearest in line was William Henry Jocelyn, a fifty-five-year-old retired sea captain and bachelor, grandson of the second earl by his second marriage. Fortunately for Tollymore and the other Roden estates, the turn of the century was relatively uneventful in Ireland. England was now more pre-occupied with events overseas, and the political factions in Ireland were biding their time, or disputing amongst themselves. Any manifestation of discontent was largely confined to industrial conditions in the major towns and cities.

There was little inclination on the part of the elderly incumbents of Tollymore to move with the times and find a productive use for the Land Act windfalls. Being unable or unwilling to adapt to the new circumstances, they stood back and let matters take their course. The fine art collection that had been assembled with

Portrait of John Strange Jocelyn by G. F. Clarke, 1856, dressed in the uniform of the Scots Fusiliers. He became the fifth Earl of Roden in 1880

great care and taste by Lord Limerick, the second Earl of Clanbrassill and the early Rodens, augmented by numerous inheritances, could still be seen at Tollymore; but it would soon fragment. Of uniformly high quality, it encompassed furniture, pictures, silver, sculpture and books. Two still-life pictures by Frans Snyders were part of a set of four, the remaining two hanging at the Hermitage in St Petersburg. Important works by Zuccarelli and Teniers were likewise displayed in the main reception rooms. On special occasions guests dined off solid silver plates, part of a set of sixty-four pieces made by the leading 18th-century silversmiths Pierre Platel and Jonathan Sage. All of these were dispersed. In due course a first folio of Shakespeare's plays and other important books would find their way to the Folger Library in Washington. The Frick Collection in New York takes pride in its two Clanbrassill pictures.[48] A selection of important books was snapped up by local dealers; some had been acquired by Viscount Jocelyn, Lord Chancellor of

Ireland and father of the first Earl of Roden, in the sale of Dean Swift's personal library in 1745.[49] Pictures, silver and other fine art that were once at Tollymore are now on view in museums and institutions across the world. Items were sold at random and for little purpose at a time when prices were a collector's waking dream. That they are now kept for posterity and were not burnt to ashes in the 1878 fire is a credit to those who risked their lives to save them.

When the third earl's eldest son, Robert Jocelyn, died of cholera, much of the panache, energy and excitement generated by the younger members of the family vanished from Tollymore. The tall, good-looking young officer in the Rifle Brigade had been a much-needed counterbalance to his stern Evangelical father. In his old age, the third earl had become an even more austere autocrat. His grand-daughter, Mabell, Countess of Airlie, remembered being brought to Tollymore for her holidays:

> *We loved the picnics in the Mourne Mountains and digging for sand eels on the seashore at Dundrum. The high jaunting cars which my grandmother always used were a joy to us, although when we first went to Tollymore we were so small that stools were put into the well in the middle of the car for us, as we would have rolled off the ordinary seats. There were other delights too - our own tiny strips of garden in which we grew mustard and cress, to be presented with great pride to the grown-ups at their late breakfast; the home farm where we helped to mix the pigs' food; the carpenter's shop where we were allowed as a special treat to make dolls' furniture.*

But even as a child she was aware of the cold, restrained atmosphere of the household:

> *Even in the relaxed holiday atmosphere of Tollymore religion had a prominent place in our daily lives. There were morning and evening prayers every day in the chapel, which served in addition to its sacred functions as a centre of practical Christianity. It was always well heated, weekdays and Sundays, and anyone homeless and in need of a night's lodging was given a meal and allowed to sleep there. Sometimes whole families would be seated on the benches, disposing of hard-boiled eggs, thick slabs of bread and butter and steaming plates of soup. Sundays were observed on strict Sabbatarian lines; no cooking was done, no games were played. In the morning, between breakfast and church, our governess read to us from the Bible or Pilgrim's Progress. On Sunday afternoons we were*

> *permitted books with a religious bias, such as lives of the missionaries, or descriptions of the Holy Land, and after tea Grandmother read a sermon to us, a privilege received with anything but gratitude. In her eyes duty to God was represented by churchgoing, duty to one's neighbour by visiting the sick and caring for the poor. Every day at luncheon the butler used to bring into the dining-room three or four baskets tightly fitted with gallipots, and into them were ladled the remains of the most succulent dishes, to be taken to the invalids. We children used to cast wistful eyes on our favourite puddings as they were whisked off the table, but we had to be content with a mere taste. Any request for a second helping would have been met with a homily on self-indulgence. With appetites still unsatisfied we used to set out immediately after luncheon, on foot or in the jaunting car, to deliver the gallipots to the chosen recipients.*[50]

Although the religious zeal gradually faded away with the demise of the third earl, and his chapel-cum-hostel was turned into an upstairs kitchen, the more dour aspects of Victorian life had become fossilised in the draughty corridors and halls of the second earl's mansion, never to leave them.

The sea-captain earl died in 1910, the same year as Edward VII, Tollymore passing to yet another elderly relation. This was his brother Robert Julian Jocelyn, who was by then sixty-five, a retired army colonel who had seen service in the Zulu war thirty years previously. At least he had a son and heir, but he lived just long enough to complete his brother's estate and pay the death duty before he too died in 1915.[51] His son Robert, the eighth earl, along with his family came to Tollymore at the beginning of the first World War and left at the very nadir of the second.

1. Robert Jocelyn, first Earl of Roden (1721-1797), succeeded to the baronetcy of his kinsman Sir Conyers Jocelyn, fourth baronet, in 1778. He was created Earl of Roden of High Roding, Co. Tipperary, in 1771. The Jocelyn family originally came from France. In 1146, Gilbert Jocelyn founded the order of the Gilbertines in Lincolnshire, and was made a saint in 1202. Robert, first Viscount Jocelyn, father of the first earl of Roden and one time Lord Chancellor of Ireland, was the first member of the family known to have come to Ireland. He lived in Donnybrook Castle (Ballinguile), Co. Dublin, a remarkable late 16th-century house, which he had acquired in 1726; see Peter Harbison (2004) *Beranger's Rambles in Ireland*, pp75-76. In 1741 he leased Mount Merrion house from the fifth Viscount Fitzwilliam.
2. Roden (ed.) 1870. *Diary of Anne Countess Dowager of Roden.* Louisa and Harriot were her daughters. General Nugent was preparing for the Battle of Ballynahinch which took place a few days later.

3. Roden Papers. Estate Accounts.
4. Roden Papers. John Jocelyn to his mother Anne Dowager Countess of Roden (19.8.1801). John Jocelyn of Brockley Park, Co. Leix (see note 8 below), fourth son of the first Earl of Roden, followed his elder brother, George, as MP for Dundalk from 1798 to 1800. He then represented Louth from 1800 to 1810 and again from 1820 to 1826. After the Act of Union the number of MPs returned for Dundalk was reduced from two to one. Aware of the importance of the Borough to the family, they carefully avoided any serious confrontations such as those that had beset the second Earl of Clanbrassill. The Jocelyn family maintained their control over the Dundalk political scene until the Reform Act of 1832 which introduced greater voter representation.
5. Roden Papers. Charles Moore to Anne Dowager Countess of Roden (8.6.1801).
6. Portrait of Anne, Countess of Roden, in the Roden Collection.
7. Rt Hon. Robert Jocelyn, second Earl of Roden (1756-1820), sat as MP for Dundalk 1783-90-7. Unlike the second Earl of Clanbrassill, he voted for the Union and was made a representative peer. Johnston-Liik (2002) *op.cit.*, vol. IV, p492.
8. Brockley Park, Co. Leix (formerly Queen's County), was a three-storey, seven-bay house with outstanding interiors. It was stripped in 1944, but little now remains.
9. Hyde Hall, Hertfordshire, continued in the family until the death of the fifth Earl of Roden's widow in 1916.
10. Roden Papers. Lady Caroline Jocelyn to Robert, Viscount Jocelyn (23.12.1806). The second Earl of Roden married, firstly (1788), Frances Theodosia, eldest daughter of the Very Rev. Robert Bligh, dean of Elphin, and niece of the first Earl of Darnley. He married, secondly (1804), Juliana Orde, youngest daughter of John Orde, Weetwood, Northumbria. By his second marriage he had two more sons; when the fifth Earl of Roden died without an heir in 1897, the present Roden line descended from the elder of these sons.
11. Roden Papers. John Straton to Viscount Jocelyn (22.1.1805). General John Straton was married to Lady Emelia Jocelyn, daughter of the first Earl of Roden. The location of Pepys Cottage has not been identified; it is unlikely to have been the 'Visitors Dining Room', close to the river near the hermitage, for this structure is not depicted on the 1834 Ordnance Survey map.
12. In the Roden Papers there is a map of this small deer park, surveyed in February 1805 by Stephen Gribbin, at a scale of 20 perches to an inch (see illustration on page 98). It states that the park area was 40 acres, 1 rood, 17 perches in Irish Plantation measure - the equivalent to 65 statute acres or 26.3 hectares.
13. There is a good example of such a deer park still existing at Crom, County Fermanagh; Reeves-Smyth (1997b) 'The natural history of demesnes', in J.W. Foster and H.C.G. Chesney (eds.), *Nature in Ireland: A Scientific and Cultural History*, p564.
14. Until the repeal of the glass tax, small panes were much cheaper than large ones. They were also less likely at this time to be pitted and uneven and consequently less susceptible to frost damage.
15. Reilly (1839) *op. cit.*
16. The Fencibles were involved at Gibbets Rath, on the Curragh, where a large number of insurgents were killed in an encounter with Government forces. The insurgents were in the

process of negotiating surrender terms. The regimental standards hung in the main stair-well at Tollymore.

17. In 1803, the Rodens' total debt had risen to £103,000, an enormous sum at that time. This was supported by a landed income of £14,000. Sinecures, such as Auditor-General and political control of Dundalk, were essential if the family was to avoid bankruptcy.

18. Ulster was England's main supplier of cattle. Reared in the hill farms, including the Mournes, they were driven to Donaghadee for shipment. Between 1801 and 1811 Belfast's population rose by 47% due to the demand for labour in the mills. In 1810 Belfast exported 15 million yards of linen, much of it for ship's sails and tents. Bust followed boom, and a severe trade depression ensued after the end of the Napoleonic Wars.

19. Roden Papers. James Jocelyn to his brother, Robert (27.8.1804).

20. Roden Papers. Letters of the third Earl of Roden. The Evangelical Movement was given added impetus by the French Revolution and the Irish 1798 Rebellion. In 1831 it was proposed that education should be non-denominational. The Evangelical Movement pulling in one direction and O'Connell's decision to politicize the education issue sadly brought the concept to a halt. The third earl was the last of the earls to use Dundalk House, and was quite active in the town. He advanced money towards the completion of the harbour works and participated in the new railway ventures.

21. Roden Papers. Lt-Col. John Strange Jocelyn to his father, the third Earl of Roden (7.12.1854 and 18.3.1855). As a front-line officer in the Scots Fusilier Guards (afterwards the Scots Guards), Strange Jocelyn participated in all the major Crimean battles. His letters from the Crimea were published in *With the Guards We Shall Go* by The Countess of Airlie. He was also featured in a television documentary on the Crimean War. Some commentators consider him to be the father of John Strange Churchill, Winston Churchill's brother but, apart from the similarity of Christian names, there is nothing to substantiate this. Irish participation in the British army at the time of the Crimea War is estimated to have been 40%, see Brian Griffin (2001). 'Ireland and the Crimea War'. *The Irish Sword*, XXII (No.89), p281.

22. Elizabeth Bowen (1942) *Bowen's Court*.

23. *Tollymore Park Guide* (1955), p9.

24. The use of heavy draft horses continued in the forests throughout the 20th century. Close to the Old Bridge is a boulder inscribed to the memory of David Stewart who is regarded as the father of state forestry in Northern Ireland.

25. Charlotte Elizabeth Tonna (1838) *Letters from Ireland in 1837*, p236.

26. Roden Papers. Memorandum addressed to 'around the breakfast table' dated 26th September, 1833.

27. An oak sapling from Tollymore was chosen as the representative oak tree for the National Memorial Arboretum at Alrewas near Birmingham. The Arboretum was conceived as a living tribute to the wartime generations of the 20th century. In it the Irish Infantry Grove commemorates the sacrifices made by the Irish Infantry Regiments of The Line throughout history.

28. The New Deer Park continued to be known as such, even though the deer had been moved to their new quarters between the house and the Barbican Gate. Parnell's Bridge is said to have been named after Sir John Parnell, the great-grandfather of Charles Stuart Parnell. The

links between the families went back to the first Earl of Roden and his children. However, in the circumstances, it is more likely that the third earl named the bridge, several roads and Parnell's View after one of Sir John's grandsons, the Rev. George Parnell. Hore's Bridge, which was built in 1824, is named after the Hore family from Wexford. Harriet Jocelyn, a niece of the second earl, married the Rev. Walter Hore, rector of Ferns, Co. Wexford (died 1843).

29. The third Earl of Roden (1788-1870) married firstly (1813), Maria Frances Catherine, daughter of Thomas Lord Le Despencer; and, secondly (1862), Clementina Janet, widow of Capt. Robert Lushington Reilly of Scarvagh, County Down.
30. The Mission's official history was written by Laurence Oliphant. *Narrative of the Earl of Elgin's Mission to China and Japan in the years 1857, 1858, & 1859.*
31. Lord Jocelyn (1841) *Six Months with the Chinese Expedition*. Viscount Jocelyn was Military Secretary to the Chinese Mission.
32. Lady Frances (Fanny) Cowper was Lady of the Bedchamber and a close friend of Queen Victoria, herself a collector of photographs. In 1841 Frances married Robert Viscount Jocelyn, the third earl's eldest son (1816-1854). Collections of her photographs are in the National Gallery of Australia and the Victoria & Albert Museum. She often skilfully montaged her photographs to create telling images of her life and relationships, while the high quality of her photographs owed much to her grasp of the chemicals and metals used in those days. She died in 1880.
33. Charlotte Elizabeth Tonna (1838) *Letters from Ireland in 1837*, pp152 & 188.
34. The Barbican gate lodge was demolished in the late 1960s.
35. J. Birch (1879) *Picturesque Lodges*. He specialised in cottage designs and was known as a pioneer in the use of concrete.
36. Roden Papers. The Rev. Walter Hore to the third Earl of Roden (26.1.1841), and Captain Hill, the agent, to the third Earl of Roden in January 1841. There is no record of where the ice-house stood.
37. Relief Committees were particularly active in County Down. The Bryansford Committee, as recorded in a letter from the chairman, looked after the worst affected by, 'cheapening [food] to those whose wages ... cannot enable them to purchase provisions at the exorbitant rates of the markets and the huxters'. Ulster landlords tended to waive much of the rent due, even though the burden for often lavish and questionable public works fell on them through the Poor Law levies. The British Government contributed less then half the cost of famine relief in Ireland, the balance being raised in the country itself. By comparison, ten times as much money was spent on the Crimean War a few years later. The desperate winter of 1846/7 brought most relief work to a standstill, causing devastation to ill-clad and famished workers. Rathfriland and some of the western Mourne areas were badly affected, yet south-eastern, coastal areas the other side of the mountains from Tollymore escaped more lightly.
38. The route through Dolly's Brae was a long one, and the police were concerned that the march might provoke the local inhabitants. The Orangemen had been armed by the authorities following recent insurrections. The lenient treatment of the Orangemen afterwards, for which the third earl lost his position as Justice of the Peace, further polarised feelings in the post-famine era.

39. B. Noel (1837). *Notes on a Short Tour through the Midland Counties of Ireland in 1836 with Observations on the Conditions of the Peasantry.*
40. He sat as Conservative MP for King's Lynn from 1842 until his death in 1854.
41. Robert Viscount Jocelyn, aged only thirty-eight, died in the home of Viscount Palmerston in Carlton Gardens, where he called on his way to his own residence at Kew. His widow, Frances, died twenty-five years later having spent most of her life at Queen Victoria's court. Her mother's second marriage was to Henry John Temple, third Viscount Palmerston, who served as Prime Minister almost continuously from 1855 to his death in 1865. See also note 32 above.
42. The advent of strychnine in the 1830s caused the loss of many raptors throughout Ireland.
43. Christine Hardyment (1997) *Behind the Scenes: Domestic Arrangements in Historic Houses*, pp177-8.
44. The fourth Earl of Roden was attending the funeral of the King of Italy as a representative of Queen Victoria to whom he was a Lord-in-Waiting. There were three servants and a housekeeper in the house at the time. The central block contained a reception room, the library and the two main bedrooms above. Fortunately, only one person was slightly injured: the estate carpenter, James Rooney, received a cut in the eye while fighting the fire on the roof.
45. James Rawson Carroll (circa 1830-1911), who commenced his own practice in 1857, was based at 176 Great Brunswick Street. He is credited by the *Irish Builder* with an extensive country house practice (1911, p858, obituary). This included Classiebawn, County Sligo, commissioned in 1874 for the Hon. William F. Cowper-Temple of Broadlands, a half-brother of the fourth Earl of Roden's mother.
46. The most spectacular example of the French château manner in Ulster was William Barre's 1860s remodelling of Roxborough Castle, County Tyrone (burnt in 1922).
47. The wife of John Strange, fifth Earl of Roden, was the Hon. Sophia Hobhouse, daughter and co-heir of John Cam, first Lord Broughton. The marriage took place in 1851.
48. The two Frick Collection pictures are the Countess of Clanbrassill (first creation) by Anthony Van Dyke and a *trompe l'oeil* by Jean-Etienne Liotard.
49. Viscount Jocelyn was the first Governor of Swift's Hospital in Dublin, nowadays more usually known as St Patrick's Hospital. He was also President of the Dublin Physico-Historical Society.
50. The Countess of Airlie (1962) *Thatched with Gold*, p5
51. The seventh earl married (1882) Ada Maria, daughter of Col. Soame Gambier Jenyns.

*CHAPTER 6*

# The Later Years

After their wedding in 1905, the future eighth Earl of Roden and his wife were drawn in style, sitting on a gig, to the front of Tollymore House by the tenants and employees. (One of those in the group was Nicolas Douglas, the head-gardener, who worked for no less than five Roden earls.[1]) But this time the portents looked more promising. The heir was only twenty-three and his wife, Elinor, came from the Parr banking dynasty. When his father, the seventh earl, had moved into Tollymore in 1910, Robert settled in what was once the Roden Arms in Bryansford village and became familiar with the estate. He had also attended an agricultural college in England. He seemed groomed for the job of eventually running Tollymore and the remaining family estates.

However, in August 1914 he received his mobilization papers and reported for duty with the North Irish Horse, shortly afterwards setting off for France with a detachment of men, many of whom came from the surrounding district. They left from Dublin's North Wall in company with the South Irish Horse. Both regiments were Special Reserve Cavalry Regiments more involved in general support work than front-line trench warfare. Nevertheless, the eighth earl saw service in the retreat from Mons and the advance from the Marne to the Aisne. In 1916, he was invalided out, spending months in English nursing homes before rejoining his regiment at their depot in Antrim. His health didn't improve and he was formally discharged in 1917. He was more fortunate than many of his generation. The losses in the first, and later in the second World War, were losses that a small country like Ireland could ill afford.

While he was still serving in France, his father died. The eighth earl's wife and young family duly moved from the village into the main house, where he joined them on his return. The countess's diary during the war years followed the actions in France and recorded difficulties travelling to England. 'We had to go by Larne and Stranraer. No other steamers were going on account of a submarine which had been laying mines'. But when they got to London they were bombed by Zeppelin airships:

> We were woken up by the housemaid and told to go into the corridor on the first floor. Most amusing sights. The Pennyfeathers in jewels and evening dress just back from the opera. Others in night-gowns and curling papers. I refused to go down and watched from my window.

While her husband was receiving specialist medical treatment, the countess worked in a canteen at Woolwich; '500 girls, munitions workers, came in for dinner and tea'. On the journey back to Ireland their ship was 'accompanied by two airships, a destroyer and three patrol boats'. Sandwiched between entries about the progress of the war were recurring items of Irish news, particularly the growing activities of Sinn Féin. Then, *'November 11th. 1918.* The Armistice signed. I heard the great news riding back from hunting near Dundrum'. When the Peace Treaty was finally ratified there were massive celebrations throughout the country. 'A huge bonfire in the Monument field and sports around it. We burnt an effigy of the Kaiser on top of the bonfire. A lovely night and we could see two fires on the Isle of Man'.

After the war that was meant to end all wars came to an end, and families tried to come to terms with the losses of relations and loved ones, attention focused on political issues in Ireland. The Irish Home Rule Bill had received the Royal Assent on September 18th 1914 but was suspended for twelve months, or for the duration of the war whichever was the longer. The war was not as short a war as everyone thought it would be, and the moderates in the Irish Party were unable to capitalize on their pre-war political gains. After the 1916 Rising, prisoners were led away from the centre of Dublin to muted booing. But a year later, after public opinion had swung in favour of the Sinn Féin movement, some of those same prisoners were returned at by-elections with resounding victories. In the general election after the 1918 Armistice, the first in eight years, Sinn Féin had an overwhelming majority. This democratic success brought little acknowledgement from England, or indeed America, who were fully occupied with the peace negotiations at Versailles. But violence, which broke out the following year, certainly had the effect of concentrating London's attention. By 1920, Sinn Féin's attempt to establish an independent state through political means had deteriorated into guerrilla warfare between English auxiliaries and armed nationalists, with the ordinary people of Ireland caught in between. As neither side was capable of an outright victory, a truce was agreed in July 1921 as a prelude to peace negotiations. The Treaty, signed in December that year, effectively gave 26 counties of Ireland Dominion status. A separate Northern Irish Parliament, based at Stormont, had already been created in 1920. The partition of Ireland was now an accepted fact. However, the Treaty was rejected by the less pragmatic of the nationalist interests and civil war ensued. Probably more than any other factor, the Civil War brought down a barrier between the six counties of Northern Ireland and the rest of the country. It was a barrier that also divided the Roden estates.[2]

There had been evidence of Sinn Féin activity in and around Tollymore during the war. The Tricolour was flown from the chalet on the Tea House Hill, whereupon the eighth earl promptly dynamited the little tea-house and nearby stables. Strikes, along with attacks on barracks and neighbouring estates, were part and parcel of life in County Down in the early 1920s. Yet people went about their everyday business amid the political turmoil and periodic, armed engagements. Tennis tournaments, shooting parties and dances took place in a Bowenesque atmosphere of uncertainty and unreality. *February 14th 1921. Hunted from Ballykinlar past interned Sinn Féiners, some of whom had stopped us hunting last year*'. And again. 'Went to a delightful dance at Ballykinlar. We all had to come back in a convoy [of] about 20 motors. We found an armoured tender in Newcastle waiting to escort us up to Tollymore'.

Raids for arms were common occurrences. 'William Skillen from the mountain arrested and taken to Victoria Barracks. He had been raided by Sinn Féiners and they had taken two rifles from him. Illegal to possess rifles. They had also raided old Turner and taken a rifle and a revolver from him'. Instead of retaining arms for their own protection, the men living in and around Tollymore were encouraged to hand in their weapons and join the Special Constabulary. 25 guns were duly handed in and a squad of 15 men formed the nucleus of the local 'B' Special unit. Shortly afterwards Tollymore was singled out for attention:

> *May 31st 1922. Attack on Tollymore. Heard at 11.30 p.m. that seventy men were coming. Roden out on patrol at the time so I sent the messenger, Willie Douglas, to retrieve him if possible, and organised the maids and Betty* [her daughter] *for defence. They watched at the windows with shotguns and rifles. Miss Wood* [the newly-arrived governess] *had the bomb. We always had one or two of these handy. It was very dark so we couldn't distinguish friend from foe and dared not shoot. Roden returned and shot at three men in the Drying Green, then ran down to the rockery from where a lot were advancing, and hurled a bomb at them. The men shot at parties in the garden and Monument field, then took the garden in*

Armoured car at Tollymore during the early 1920s

*line and cleared it. By 3.30am all was over and the attack frustrated. They tried to break in at the garden door but it had been sandbagged a week ago. The rest was steel shuttered.*

Not all skirmishes ended so satisfactorily. Whilst on patrol near the sawmill, James Skillen, a relative of the William Skillen arrested for keeping two rifles, was accidentally shot by another member of the 'B' Specials. He was brought back to the house and later given a full military funeral. He appears to have been the only serious casualty at Tollymore on either side.

The countess was able to record in her diary at the beginning of 1923, 'all quiet in the North of Ireland and Roden resigns from the B Constabulary'. It was a changed life but a relatively peaceful one. The main concerns were now dock and rail strikes which threatened the supply of basic foodstuffs. However, one aspect of life at Tollymore which appears to have remained undisturbed by all these events was the austere routine of the main house, a routine punctuated by the arrival of the occasional guest and the annual dance for the staff and their families. The Clanbrassill Barn had been turned into a theatre by the eighth earl's mother during her brief tenure at Tollymore. Surprised guests were sometimes press-ganged into learning their parts in double-quick time for the weekend's performance. Before she came to Tollymore in 1910, she had published a number of novels which took as their theme life in large houses and on the hunting field.[3] Turning to the theatre, she wrote and produced plays at Tollymore and on one occasion brought them to London for a season. In her own way she may have tried, but she had been unable to lift the oppressive veil that enveloped the house, a house largely unchanged since the days of the second earl.

The children of Tollymore, who should have been allowed to roam with carefree abandon through the forests and mountains, were brought up in a régime that was strict even by the standards of those days. If they wanted to fish on the rivers or lake, which once held a good stock of brown trout, they had to ask permission, a permission that was not always forthcoming - 'for their own good'. A visiting journalist from *The Times* did his best to put a gloss on life at Tollymore in an article entitled 'The Peace of the Old Days':

> *Now that the affairs in Ulster have settled down again after the Irish revolution and the bad times, there is something of the old peace and quietness in the life of the country family. It was a big house in which we stayed, and all around us were hill and woods. There was only one narrow, bumpy road leading from the town to the lodge gates. But inside the house, life proceeded in an easy, well-regulated manner. Everything was extremely and nicely unmodern, as though the family had failed entirely to move with the times. This atmosphere of days before the War was noticeable in different ways. There was in the first place none of the luxury of modern times, and in the second place none of the Philistinism. Though the house was very large there were only three bathrooms, and the guests were sent to bed with candles which flickered uneasily down the long dark galleries; we heaved a nightly sigh of relief when the bedroom door was reached and safely closed behind us. Modern electric light, though we cannot live for long without it, by taking away the mystery of the darkness has deprived our houses of so much of their character.*
>
> *To counteract the lack of light there was the excellence of the food, which was served and eaten with a punctuality unknown to most of the big houses in England. Even at breakfast and tea the host and hostess would wait till their guests were assembled before entering the dining-room. The family was very orderly and well-behaved. The head of the family was obeyed; the children were seen and not heard. The house was rather cold, and there was only one fire in the billiard room, where we all congregated.*

> *The excellent billiard-table was also treated with reverence; no running games of fives or pockets were allowed, only billiards. After luncheon we took walks of inspection round the demesne; any thought of taking out the car and driving to the nearest cinema would have been considered highly out of place. The town was rarely visited, except on business, by any of the family. After dinner we played cards and retired early to bed. That this quiet, uneventful life exercises a peculiar fascination was revealed to us by the words and attitudes of our host and hostess. There are but few neighbours round about, and one or two visitors a year are all the company they enjoy. Yet so strong is the attraction of the place and surroundings that our hostess, after taking her little boy to school in England, wasted no time but travelled home again by the next boat, to resume her life of isolation among the hills and green fields.*[4]

The family's life at Tollymore was not quite as isolated as *The Times* journalist was led to believe. It may have appeared Spartan to the visitor, but the eighth earl compensated himself and his wife with extensive travel. When foreign travel was not as frequent as today, the countess recorded holidays in the West Indies, Europe, and the Middle East; interspersed with cruises and visits to relations in England for shooting parties. It may have been the lifestyle the eighth earl considered more appropriate to an Irish Representative Peer at Westminster, but it was not conducive to the successful management of the family's estates. The Flaitha, or nobles, of the Magennis clans would have begun to have misgivings about the earl's stewardship of their ancient townlands. For whatever reason - it may have been his health, the unsettled state of the country or the burdensome structure of the main house - he gradually set his face against Ireland. For once, Tollymore had failed to weave its magic. After the final payments had been received under the Land Acts, the eighth earl was comfortably off. His wife, who was financially independent, contributed to the garden and the running of the large establishment she liked to keep. Yet he avoided any further development of the land and forests within the demesne, or indeed the outlying farms. Throughout the 1920s, he actively sought buyers for the adjoining properties and, when none appeared, tried auctions with little better result. In June 1929, just a few months before the Wall Street Crash, he completed the sale of the first tranche of forestry to the Northern Ireland Government. Partly due to the heavy felling during the first World War and the lack of funds for public afforestation, the price paid was just over £6 per acre. Even so it absorbed most of the Forestry Service's budget. The land in question was most of the area south of the river and included the plantations so assiduously laid out by Lord Limerick and his son, the Earl of Clanbrassill. Following the sale, the countess recorded in her diary, 'we [now] possess nothing but the house and grounds'.

The 1930s did see some minor changes to the demesne, The Wooden Bridge was built downstream from the Hermitage to replace the Suspension Bridge. Various farm and garden buildings were demolished, among them the stables and melon houses - all surplus to requirements. The countess was an active gardener, planting numerous trees and shrubs in the arboretum and elsewhere. She was also responsible for renewing some of the beech woods along the river.

Both the earl's sons had been encouraged to join the Navy, a career that in those days started in the early teens and involved service in every ocean of the world, but not one to prepare an heir for estate management in the fullness of time. Yet the brothers always maintained a deep attachment to Tollymore, returning when postings and holidays permitted. In 1937, the elder son, Robert William, married Clodagh Kennedy of Bishops Court, County Kildare. Like his parents before him, they duly made their home at Bryansford.

But from now on, home leave would become more restricted as storm clouds once again gathered across Europe and another war appeared inevitable. The countess's diary mentions hurried visits to London and relations. Everywhere there was a general air of tension. In May 1939 Tollymore was offered to the Government as a hospital. Dr Robb and a matron from Downpatrick hospital came to see the house, followed shortly afterwards by an inspector from the Royal Army Medical Corps. After war broke out and Germany had crushed France, Tollymore was 'measured' for a battalion of soldiers. In November 1940, two hundred and fifty members of the 179th Field Ambulance arrived. They were billeted wherever possible; in the drawing-room, library - most of the books having just been sold - even in the corridors. Meanwhile the eighth earl sectioned off part of the east wing for his own use, but it was not a very satisfactory arrangement.[5]

Unlike other owners of large houses who leased their properties to the Government for the duration of the war and moved nearby, the eighth earl re-approached the Forestry Service to see if they would acquire the remainder of Tollymore. But there was a problem. In the very depth of the war, when Germany had not yet moved against Russia and was still planning the overthrow of England, there was no money in the Northern Ireland coffers to acquire a large house and parkland, particularly as the Government already had the use of it. There were other priorities. Eventually the Minister of Agriculture, Sir Edward

Archdale, secured finance from a private source to be reimbursed at a later date, the outcome of the war permitting. What was left of the Tollymore house and demesne passed into the hands of the Forestry Service.

On November 11th 1941 the countess made a brief entry in her diary. 'We left Tollymore and came to live at Larne'. A few days afterwards she received 'a communication from the Admiralty to say that my darling John was missing, presumed killed during enemy action'. John Jocelyn, as a seventeen-year-old midshipman, had just joined the battleship, *HMS Barham*, before it was torpedoed in the Mediterranean.[6] The earl and countess then decided to move to England and went to live at Fareham outside Portsmouth. The eighth earl never returned to Ireland.

Later, when the tide of war had turned, Tollymore became a staging post for units bound for N.W. Europe. Nissen huts were put up along the main avenue to accommodate increasing numbers of personnel, while military training continued throughout the demesne and in the mountains.

After the Axis powers had been defeated and the last troops had pulled out, Tollymore House stood empty and forlorn. Large houses in the post-war era had an uncertain future, if any. At one point, the house was considered for a school, but the idea came to nothing. The only activity in the demesne was re-planting swathes of forest cut down for wartime use.[7]

In the late 1940s the eighth earl's daughter-in-law, Lady Jocelyn, realized that the centre of the house was still more or less intact. If the 19th-century extensions could be removed, the demesne opened to the public (there were then only a few, limited permits for access), and its farmland brought back into use, Tollymore could once more be made viable. On her own behalf, she entered into negotiations with the Government, who agreed to sell her that part of the property they had bought so unwillingly at the start of the war. But only on certain conditions, conditions that were beyond the bounds of normal conveyancing. The price would be the same as the purchase price, and they would have the option to buy it back, at that price, should the family ever sell it in the future. Secondly, she could not alter the structure of the main building without their prior approval. She considered the possibilities, but finally decided against taking the matter any further.[8]

In those post-war years, Government departments still wielded an authority fostered by the exigencies of wartime, rationing, high taxation and bureaucratic controls. Their policies were not for questioning. But within five years of closing the file, and with no ideas for the future of the house, the Government gave the

Foley's Bridge in winter

order for its complete demolition. The main portico and some of the cut granite were removed before the rest was reduced to rubble.⁹ The heart of the demesne, with its history and many local and world-wide associations, was scattered over the forest roads in need of repair.

The year 1953 saw the passing of the Forestry Act, which became a defining milestone in forestry management. Included in the Act was a declaration of areas to be designated as future National Forest Parks. The Forestry Service was now aware that, in addition to the extraction of timber - the greater part of which was from original demesnes - they had in their portfolio properties of considerable importance that could become valuable resources for leisure activities.

The decision was taken to create the first such forest park at Tollymore. Accompanied by the Minister of Agriculture and to a salute from the band of the King's Own Scottish Borderers, the Governor of Northern Ireland, Lord Wakehurst, declared Tollymore Park open to the public on 2ⁿᵈ June 1955. In that first year alone, there were over 30,000 visitors, increasing over a ten-year period to nearly 150,000 per annum. So popular was the demesne, that at one point there was a question whether Tollymore could absorb the growing number of visitors. But it did, many of them coming for repeat visits. Car parks were built on the site of the house and kitchen gardens. Walks were marked out, more wooden bridges and stepping-stones were put across the rivers. Caravanning and camping arrangements were laid out, catering facilities built, all to look after the growing demand for a variety of leisure activities. Mountaineers, who had been looking for a base in the Mournes, at first used part of the ninth earl's house in Bryansford before the purpose-built Mountain Centre was opened in the 1970s close to Tollymore's West Gate. Over the succeeding years several climbers who had been introduced to the sport at Tollymore went on to climb or lead expeditions to all the highest mountains in the world, including Mount Everest.

Many people down the years have expressed their feelings about Tollymore. Lord Limerick's guest, Edward Walpole, would have written 'a poetical sketch of the whole place', if he had not 'stuffed himself with venison and mutton'. In the following century, Edward Lear found Tollymore 'full of beautiful ruins and bridges and trees and roads and hills and mills and lawns and laurels'.[10] In a less lyrical vein, Peter Rankin, in the Ulster Architectural Heritage Society's 1975 work on the Mournes, considered, 'Tollymore [to be] arguably the finest eighteenth century demesne in the north of Ireland, its estate and garden buildings and structures both in quality and quantity rivalled only by those at Hillsborough and Downhill, its picturesque qualities rivalled by neither'.[11]

In one form or another the same sentiments were echoed by the people of Ireland in a market survey commissioned in 1964 to assess the views of visitors and establish where they came from, what their backgrounds were and how many times they visited the Park. The peace and tranquillity of the demesne rated most highly. It was 'restful and refreshing to weary spirits'. But there were other reasons for a visit, like the case of a young girl who 'wanted to be alone with my boyfriend'. And the response from a somewhat harassed visitor. 'Don't know yet, the CIE bus should have gone to Armagh'![12]

Whatever the reasons for visiting Tollymore, and there are many, the scenery that first caught Lord Limerick's attention, and which he and his son so carefully enhanced, will continue to attract and beguile all those who enter through the Earl of Clanbrassill's gate lodges and let their attention wander out over the river valley and forests towards the Mourne Mountains beyond. Lord Limerick's original demesne, after all the vicissitudes of history, lives on as a Forest Park that is now enjoyed by many thousands of families from Ireland, and all over the world.

1. A handsome silver trophy, won by Nicolas Douglas at a 1906 horticultural show, was presented to the forest park by his niece, May Coffin, and can be seen in the Clanbrassill Barn, now a museum.
2. Dundalk House was pulled down in 1909 to make way for offices, and Dundalk demesne sold in 1920.
3. Before becoming the Countess of Roden, she wrote under her married name Mrs Robert Jocelyn. When her son inherited, she went to live firstly in Bryansford, then in England until her death in 1931.
4. *The Times* article was written sometime between 1922 and 1927 when electric light was installed.
5. The Roden Papers. The Countess of Roden's Diary - September 14th, 1940.
6. John Jocelyn was the younger son of the eighth Earl of Roden. When *HMS Barham* was torpedoed it sank within minutes. It is now known that John, although injured, managed to get off the ship but subsequently drowned. His elder brother, Robert William, who became the ninth Earl of Roden, had a distinguished naval career, rising to the rank of Captain. He served in most theatres of the second World War, including the North Atlantic, Mediterranean and the Battle of the Pacific.
7. Approximately 4,000 tons of timber, mainly high-quality larch, is now extracted from Tollymore each year.
8. Roden Papers. Correspondence between the Viscountess Jocelyn and the Northern Ireland Ministry of Agriculture 1947.
9. Much of the portico was used in 1952 to build an open air altar at Drumnaquoile, west of Seaforde, in memory of the Franciscans of the late 17th-century Friary there; see P.J. Clarke (2004) *History of a County Down Townland*, pp136-146.
10. In 1857; see A. Davidson (1950) *Edward Lear*.
11. Peter Rankin (1975) *Historic Buildings in the Mourne Area of South Down*.
12. CIE stands for Córas Iompair Éireann, the Irish national transport company.

View of
Saw Mill,
Tollymore,
circa 1865

# Bibliography

Aalen, F, Whelan, K and Stout, M. (eds). 1997. *The Atlas of the Irish Rural Landscape.* Cork: Cork University Press.

Airlie, M. Countess of. 1964. *Thatched with Gold.* London: Hutchinson.

Airlie, M. Countess of. 1933. *With the Guards We Shall Go: A Guardsman's Letters in the Crimea 1854-1855.* London: Hodder and Stoughton.

Aldrich, M. 1994. *Gothic Revival.* London: Phaidon.

Allen, G. 1793. 'A sketch of the character of Thomas Wright'. *The Gentleman's Magazine*, pp9-12; pp14-15.

Annals of Ulster. *A Chronicle of Irish Affairs from A.D. 432 to A,D. 1540.* (ed. 1887) William M. Hennessy. Four volumes. Dublin: Her Majesty's Stationary Office. Reprinted 1998 by De Búrca, Dublin.

Anon, 1834. 'Tullamore Park'. *The Dublin Penny Journal*, II (No.2), April 19th, pp348-350.

Arthington, H. 1988. 'A master of trees: architect, Thomas Wright'. *Country Life*, Feb 25th.

Atkinson, A. 1815. *The Irish Tourist.* Dublin: Author.

Atkinson, A. 1823. *Ireland Exhibited to England.* Two volumes, vol. I: Co. Down. London: Baldwin, Cradock & Joy.

Ballard, R and Archbold, R. 1987. *The Discovery of the Titanic.* London: Hodder and Stoughton.*Ballitore Magazine.* 1821. Series II.

Bardon, J. 1992. *A History of Ulster.* Belfast: Blackstaff Press.

Barnard, T. 2004. *Making the Grand Figure: Lives and Possessions in Ireland 1641-1770.* London and New Haven: Yale University Press.

Bean, W.J. 1970-1988. *Trees and Shrubs Hardy in the British Isles.* 8th edition. Four volumes, plus Supplement. London: John Murray.

Bence-Jones, M. 1974. '"A suitably Celtic twilight" Lost Irish country houses – I'. *Country Life*, vol. CLV (No.4012) 23rd May, pp1262-1264.

Bence-Jones, M. 1987. *Twilight of the Ascendancy.* London: Constable.

Bence-Jones, M. 1988. *Burke's Guide to Irish Country Houses.* London: Constable.

Bence-Jones, M. 1996. *Life in an Irish Country House.* London: Constable.

Birch, J. 1879. *Picturesque Lodges.* Edinburgh and London: W. Blackwood & Sons.

Black, E. (ed.). 1990. *Kings in Conflict: Ireland in the 1690s.* Exhibition Catalogue. Belfast: Ulster Museum.

Black, J. 1992. *The British Abroad: The Grand Tour in the Eighteenth Century.* Stroud: Sutton Publishing.

Black, J. 2003. *Italy and the Grand Tour.* New Haven and London: Yale University Press.

Boutcher, W. 1775. *A Treatise on Forest-trees.* Edinburgh: Privately printed. Irish edition 1786, Dublin: William Wilson.

Bowe, P and Lamb, K. 1995. *A History of Gardening in Ireland.* Dublin, Glasnevin: National Botanic Gardens.

Bowen, E. 1942. *Bowen's Court.* London: Longmans Green and Co.

British Travel Association. 1964. *Overseas Visitors to Northern Ireland 1963: a Survey Initiated by the British Travel and Holiday Association and the Northern Ireland Tourist Board and Planned in Co-operation with Social Surveys (Gallup Poll) Ltd.* London: British Travel Association.

Byrne, P.A. 1846. *A Picturesque Handbook to Carlingford Bay and the Watering Places in its Vicinity.* Newry.

Calender of Irish Patent Rolls of James I, see Irish Manuscripts Commission.

Carson, W. H. 1981. *The Dam Builders: The Story of the Men Who Built the Silent Valley Reservoir.* Newcastle: Mourne Observer Press.

Chart, D. A (ed.). 1940. *A Preliminary Survey of the Ancient Monuments of Northern Ireland. Belfast*: His Majesty's Stationary Office.

Christie, C. 2000. *The British Country House in the Eighteenth Century.* Manchester and New York: Manchester University Press.

Clanbrassill (see Hamilton)

Clark, K. 1928. *The Gothic Revival. An Essay in the History of Taste.* London: Constable (second edition 1950: John Murray).

Clarke, P.J. 2004. *History of a County Down Townland. Drumaroad.* Drumaroad: Patrick Clarke.

Colvin, H. 1995. *A Biographical Dictionary of British Architects. 1600-1840.* 3rd edition. New Haven and London: Yale University Press.

Craig, M. 1976. *Classic Houses of the Middle Size.* London and New York: The Architectural Press and Architectural Book Publishing.

Crowe, W.H. 1968. *The Ring of Mourne.* Dundalk: Dundalgan Press.

Cust, L. 1898. *History of the Society of Dilettanti.* S. Colvin (ed.). London: Macmillan. Reprinted with additions, 1914.

Daniels, S. 1999. *Humphry Repton: Landscape Gardening and the Geography of Georgian England.* New Haven and London: Yale University Press.

Davidson, A. 1950. *Edward Lear.* New York: Penguin.

Dean, J. A.K. 1994. *The Gate Lodges of Ulster.* Belfast: Ulster Architectural Heritage Society.

Deane, D. 1983. *The Ulster Countryside.* Belfast: Century Books.

De Breffny, B. 1987. 'Liotard's Irish paintings'. *Irish Arts Review*, 4, No. 2, (Summer), pp31-38.

[Department] Ministry of Agriculture Northern Ireland. 1955. *Tollymore Park Guide.* Belfast, HMSO.

Department of Agriculture Northern Ireland (Forest Service). 1964. *Tollymore Forest Park.* Guide. Belfast: HMSO.

Department of Agriculture Northern Ireland (Forest Service). 1972. *Tollymore Forest Park.* Guide. Belfast: HMSO.

Department of Agriculture Northern Ireland (Forest Service). Not dated but circa 1985. *Tollymore Forest Park.* Guide. Belfast: HMSO.

Desmond, R. 1994. *Dictionary of British and Irish Botanists and Horticulturists*. London: Taylor and Francis with the Natural History Museum.

Dingwall, C and Aldridge, D. 1999. *The Hall of Mirrors. Reflections on the Sublime and on the Iconography of Ossian at the Hermitage, Dunkeld*. New Arcadian Journal, No. 47/48. Leeds, Patrick Eyres.

Dooley, T. 2001. *The Decline of the Big House in Ireland*. Dublin: Wolfhound Press.

Dooley, T. 2003. *A Future for Irish Historic Houses: A Study of Fifty Houses*. Dublin, Irish Georgian Society.

Doyle, J.B. 1854. *Tours in Ulster: A Handbook to the Antiquities and Scenery of the North of Ireland*. Dublin (Reprinted in Ballynahinch: Davidson).

Dubourdieu, Rev. J. 1802. *Statistical Survey of County Down*. Dublin: Graisbery and Campbell.

Elwes, H.J and Henry, A.H. 1912. *The Trees of Great Britain and Ireland* (seven volumes 1906-1913). Edinburgh: Privately Printed (Republished 1969. Wakefield: S.R. Publishers Ltd).

Evans, E. E. 1951. *Mourne Country: Landscape and Life in South Down*. Dundalk: Dundalgan Press (Revised 1967).

Everett, N. 1999. *An Irish Arcadia: The Historic Gardens of Bantry House*. Bantry: Hafod.

Everett, N. 2001a. *Wild Gardens: The Lost Desmesnes of Bantry Bay*. Bantry: Hafod (first edition 2000).

Everett, N. 2001b. *A Landlord's Garden: Derreen, Co. Kerry*. Bantry: Hafod.

FitzGerald, O. 2001. *Ashford Castle: Through the Centuries*. Dun Laoghaire: Cadogan Publications Ltd.

Fitzpatrick, H. M. 1933. 'The trees of Ireland: native and introduced'. *Scientific Proceedings of the Royal Dublin Society*, vol. 20, pp597-656.

Fitzpatrick, W and Hawthorne, W. 1971. *Sailing Ships of Mourne*. Newcastle: Mourne Observer.

Fortescue, J. 1773. *Some Hints on Planting*. By a Planter. Newry: George Stevenson.

Four Masters. *The Annals of the Kingdom of Ireland from the Earliest Period to the Year 1616*. (ed. 1856) John O'Donovan. Seven volumes. Dublin: Hodges, Smith and Co. Reprinted 1990 by De Búrca, Dublin.

Fraser. J. 1838. *Guide through Ireland, Descriptive of its Scenery, Towns, Seats, Antiquities etc with Various Statistical Tables*. Dublin: William Curry, Jn and Co.

Glendinning, V. 1998. *Jonathan Swift*. London: Hutchinson.

Glin, The Knight of, Griffin, D. and Robinson, N. 1989. *Vanishing Country Houses of Ireland*. Dublin: Irish Architectural Archive.

Gosling, P. 1991. 'From Dún Delca to Dundalk: the topography and archaeology of a medieval frontier town, A.D. c.1187-1700'. *County Louth Archaeological and Historical Journal*, vol. 22 (No.3), pp221-353.

Griffin, B. 2001. 'Ireland and the Crimea War'. *The Irish Sword*, vol. 22 (No. 89).

Hall, S.C and Hall, A.M. 1841-3. *Ireland: Its Scenery, Character &c*. Three volumes. London: Jeremiah How.

Hamilton, J, Earl of Clanbrassill. 1783. *An Account of the Method of Raising and Planting Pinus Sylvestris, that is, Scotch Fir, or Pine, as now Practised in Scotland. Received by the Printer from the Right Honourable the Earl of Clanbrassill*. Newry: Printed by Robert Stevenson.

Hamond, F and Porter, T. 1991. *A Tour of the Mournes*. Belfast: Friar's Bush Press.

Harbison, P. 2004. *Beranger's Rambles in Ireland. Based on the Royal Irish Academy's Manuscripts 2C.31, 32 and 30*. Dublin: Wordwell.

Hardyment, C. 1997. *Behind the Scenes. Domestic Arrangements in Historic Houses.* London: The National Trust.

Harris, E. 1971a, 'The Wizard of Durham: the architecture of Thomas Wright. I'. *Country Life*, vol. CL (No.3872), Aug 26th, pp.492-495.

Harris, E. 1971b. 'A flair for the grandiose: the architecture of Thomas Wright. II'. *Country Life*, CL (No.3873), Sept 2nd, pp.546-550.

Harris, E. 1971c. 'Architect of rococo landscapes: Thomas Wright. III'. *Country Life*, CL (No.3874) Sept 9th, pp.612-615.

Harris, E. 2000. *British Architectural Books and Writers 1556-1775.* Cambridge: Cambridge University Press.

Harris, W. 1740. *Topographical and Chorographical Survey of County Down.* Dublin and London: Thomas Boreman.

Harris, W. 1744. *The Antient and Present State of the County of Down.* Dublin: Edward Exshaw (Reprinted 1977, Arthur Davidson: Ballynahinch).

Hayes, Samuel. 1794. *Practical Treatise on Planting; And Management of Woods and Coppices.* Dublin: William Sleater. Third Edition 1822, Dublin: Samuel Jones. Facsimile of first edition with foreword by Thomas Pakenham, 2003, Dublin: New Island Books.

Henrey, B. 1975. *British Botanical and Horticultural Literature Before 1800.* Three volumes. Oxford: Oxford University Press.

Hillier, H.R. 1981. *Hillier's Manuel of Trees and Shrubs.* Fifth Edition. Newton Abbot: David and Charles.

Hoare, Sir Richard Colt. 1807. *Journal of a Tour in Ireland A.D. 1806.* London: W. Miller and Dublin: Mahon.

Horner, J. 1920. *The Linen Trade of Europe during the Spinning Wheel Period.* Belfast: Linenhall Press and Oxford: McCaw, Stevenson and Orr.

Hornibrook, M. 1938. *Dwarf and Slow Growing Conifers.* London: Country Life Ltd (2nd edition also 1938)

Howley, J. 1993. *The Follies and Garden Buildings of Ireland.* New Haven and London; Yale University Press.

Hunt, W (ed.). 1907. *Irish Parliament 1775.* London: Longmans.

Ingamells, J. 1997. *A Dictionary of British and Irish Travellers in Italy 1701 - 1800. Compiled from the Brinsley Ford Archive.* New Haven and London: Yale University Press.

Irish Manuscripts Commission. 1966. *Irish Patent Rolls of James I. Facsimile of the Irish Record Commission's Calender Prepared Prior to 1830.* Foreword by M.C. Griffith. Dublin: Stationary Office.

Jackson-Stops, G. 1991. *An English Arcadia 1600-1990: Designs for Gardens and Garden Buildings in the Care of the National Trust.* London: The National Trust.

James, F.G. 1995. *Lords of the Ascendancy: The Irish House of Lords and its Members 1600 - 1800.* Dublin: Irish Academic Press.

Jocelyn, Lord R. 1841. *Six Months with the Chinese Expedition; or Leaves from a Soldier's Notebook.* London: John Murray.

Jones, B. 1953. *Follies and Grottoes.* London: Constable (2nd edition 1974).

Johnston-Liik, E.M. 2002. *The History of the Irish Parliament 1692-1800. Commons, Constituencies and Statutes.* (Six volumes). Belfast: Ulster Historical Foundation.

Jope, E. M (ed.). 1966. *Archaeological Survey of County Down.* Belfast, HMSO.

Jupp, B. 1992. *Heritage Gardens Inventory 1992*. Belfast: Northern Ireland Heritage Gardens Committee.

Kilpatrick, C. S. 1988. *Northern Ireland Forest Service: a History*. Belfast: Department of Agriculture for Northern Ireland.

Knox, A. 1875. *A History of County Down*. Dublin: Hodges, Foster & Co.

Lambert, D and Harding, S. 1989. 'Thomas Wright at Stoke Park'. *Garden History*, vol. 17, No.1 (Spring Issue), pp66-82.

Langley, B. 1747. *Gothic Architecture Improved by Rules and Proportions in many Grand Designs*. London: J. Millan.

Lear, M. 1987. The Woody Plant Catalogue – a Basis for Garden Management and Plant Conservation. MSc Thesis, University of Aberdeen.

Leinster, Emily, Duchess of. 1949. *The Correspondence of Emily, Duchess of Leinster (1731 - 1814)*. B. FitzGerald (ed.). Two volumes. Dublin: Stationary Office.

Lewis, S. 1837. *A Topography Dictionary of Ireland*. Two volumes.. London: Gilbert and Rivington.

Llanover, Lady (ed.). 1861. *The Autobiography and Correspondence of Mary Granville, Mrs Delany with Interesting Reminiscences of King George III and Queen Charlotte.*. 1700-1788 (Six volumes 1861-62). London: Richard Bentley.

Lodge, J. 1754. *The Peerage of Ireland; or, A Genealogical History of the Present Nobility of that Kingdom*. Four volumes. London: William Johnson. vol. III (Revised by Mervyn Archdall 1789 in seven volumes. Dublin: James Moore).

Loudon, J.C. 1838. *Arboretum et Fruticetum Britannicum; or, The Trees and Shrubs of Britain*. Eight volumes. London: Longmans, vol. I, pp108-10.

Loudon, J.C.1844. *Arboretum et Fruticetum Britannicum; or, The Trees and Shrubs of Britain*. Eight volumes. London: Longman, Brown, Green and Longmans, vol. IV.

Loudon, J.C. [1822] 1859. *An Encyclopaedia of Gardening* Mrs [Jane] Loudon (ed.). London: Longman, Brown, Green and Longman. New edition, London: Longman, Hurst, Rees, Orme and Brown, 1833.

Luckombe, R. 1780. *Tour through Ireland* [in 1779]. London: T. Lowndes.

Lyons, M.C. 1993. *Illustrated Incumbered Estates: Ireland, 1850 - 1905*. Whitegate: Ballinakella Press.

McCarthy, M. 1981a. 'Thomas Wright's designs for temples and related drawings for garden buildings'. *Journal of Garden History*, 1 (No.1), pp55-66.

McCarthy, M. 1981b. 'Thomas Wright's designs for gothic garden building'. *Journal of Garden History*, 1 (No3), pp239-252.

McCarthy, M. 1981c. 'Ireland ancient and modern: the architectural sketches of Thomas Wright of Durham in 1746/7'. *Connoisseur*, CCVI, pp158-161.

McCarthy, M. 1987. *The Origins of the Gothic Revival*. London and New Haven: Yale University Press.

McConville, M. 1986. *Ascendancy to Oblivion. The Story of the Anglo-Irish*. London: Phoenix Press.

McCracken, E. 1971. *The Irish Woods Since Tudor Times. Their Distribution and Exploitation*. Newton Abbot: David and Charles.

MacLochlainn, C and Lumley, I. 2004. 'Vanishing arcadia'. *An Taisce Magazine*, winter, pp16-20.

McVeagh, J. (ed.). 1995. *Richard Pocock's Irish Tours*. Dublin: Irish Academic Press.

Malcomson, A.P.W. 1969. 'The Struggle for Control of Dundalk Borough 1782 - 1792'. *County Louth Archaeological and Historical Journal*, 17 (No.1), pp22-36.

Malcomson, A.P.W. 1982. *The Pursuit of the Heiress: Aristocratic marriage in Ireland 1750 – 1820.* Belfast: Ulster Historical Foundation.

Malcomson, A.P.W. 2000. 'The Irish Peerage and the Act of Union'. *Transactions of the Royal Historical Society*, 10 (6th Series), pp289-327.

Malins, E and Glin, The Knight of. 1976. *Lost Demesnes: Irish Landscape Gardening 1660 - 1845.* London: Barrie and Jenkins.

Malins, E and Bowe, P. 1980. *Irish Gardens and Demesnes from 1830.* London: Barrie and Jenkins.

Mander, P. 1997. *The Fall and Rise of the Stately Home.* New Haven and London: Yale University Press.

Maxwell, C. 1949. *Country and Town in Ireland under the Georges.* Dundalk: William Tempest/Dundalgan Press.

Milton, T. 1783-93. *Collection of Select Views of Different Seats of the Nobility and Gentry in the Kingdom of Ireland.* London: J. Walter.

Mitchel, A. 1974. *A Field Guide to the Trees of Britain and Northern Europe.* London: Collins.

Montgomery, W. 1869. *The Montgomery Manuscripts: 1608-1706. Compiled from Family Papers, Edited with Notes by Rev. G. Hill.* Belfast: James Cleeland and Thomas Dargan.

Mowl, T. and Earnshaw, B. 1985. *A Trumpet at a Distant Gate: The Lodge as Prelude to the Country House.* London: Waterstone.

Mowl, T. and Earnshaw, B. 1999. *An Insular Rococo: Architecture, Politics and Society in Ireland and England 1710-1770.* London: Reaktion.

Neeson, E. 1991. *History of Irish Forestry.* Dublin: Lilliput.

Nelson, C. (ed.). 1982. *Northern Gardens: Gardens and Parks of Outstanding Historic Interest in Northern Ireland.* Belfast: Northern Ireland Heritage Gardens Committee.

Noel, B.W. 1837. *Notes on a Short Tour through the Midland Counties of Ireland in 1836 with Observations on the Conditions of the Peasantry.* London.

Northern Ireland Tourist Board. 1980. *Tourism in Northern Ireland.* Belfast, Northern Ireland Tourist Board (Research Department).

O'Kane, F. 2004. *Landscape Design in Eighteenth-Century Ireland.* Cork: Cork University Press.

Oliphant, L. 1859. *Narrative of the Earl of Elgin's Mission to China and Japan, 1857, 1858 & 1859.* Two volumes. London: William Blackwood & Sons. Reprinted 1970, Oxford: Oxford University Press.

*Ordnance Survey Memoirs of Ireland.* Day, A and McWilliams (eds.). *Parishes of County Down I. 1834-6. South Down.* Belfast and Dublin: The Institute of Irish Studies and the Royal Irish Academy.

O'Sullivan, H. 1967/8. 'A history of Dundalk - eighteenth century'. *Tempest's Annual.* Parts 1 & 2.

O'Sullivan, H. 1971/2. 'A history of Dundalk - nineteenth century'. *Tempest's Annual*, Parts 1 & 2.

O'Sullivan, H. 1997. 'The Magennis lordship of Iveagh in the early modern period, 1534 to 1691', in Proudfoot, L (ed.). *Down History and Society.* Dublin: Geography Publications, pp159-202.

O'Sullivan, H. 2000. *A History of Local Government in the County of Louth. From Earliest Times to the Present Time.* Dublin: Institute of Public Administration.

Pakenham, V. 2000. *The Big House in Ireland.* London: Cassell.

*Parliamentary Gazetteer of Ireland.* 1847-8. Three volumes. Dublin, London and Edinburgh: A. Fullarton.

Pococke, R. 1891. *Tour in Ireland in 1752.* G.T. Stokes (ed.). Dublin: Hodges and Figgis.

Pococke, R. 1995. *Richard Pocock's Irish Tours.* McVeagh, J. (ed.) Dublin: Irish Academic Press.

# *APPENDIX 2*

## Tree Measurements Recorded at Tollymore by Fitzpatrick in 1933

The following data has been extracted from H.M. Fitzpatrick (1933) 'The trees of Ireland: native and introduced'. *Scientific Proceedings of the Royal Dublin Society*, 20, NS 41, November 1933, pp597-656. The generally accepted botanical names for some trees listed by Fitzpatrick have changed since 1933; to avoid confusion the modern botanical name is placed in brackets, following the botanical name listed by Fitzpatrick. English names are also given where they exist.

*Abies alba*. Common Silver Fir. 104-feet x 16-feet [31.70 x 4.88 metres].
*Abies cephalonica*. Greek Fir. 70-feet x 18-feet 7-inches [21.34 x 5.66 metres].
*Abies nordmanniana*. Caucasian Fir. 60-feet [18.29 metres].
*Athrotaxis laxifolia*. Tasmanian Cedar. 12-feet [3.66 metres].
*Cedrus deodara*. Deodar Cedar. 60-feet x 9-feet 11-inches [18.29 x 2.97 metres].
*Cedrus libani*. Cedar of Lebanon. 55-feet x 16-feet 1-inch [16.76 x 4.90 metres].
*Cupressus nootkatensis* [*Chamaecyparis nootkatensis*]. Nootka Cypress. 60-feet [18.29 metres].
*Pinus pinaster*. Maritime Pine. 82-feet x 11-feet 2-inches 24.99 x 3.40 metres].
*Podocarpus chilinis* [*Podocarpus salignus*] 12-feet [3.66 metres].
*Pseudotsuga taxifolia* [*Pseudotsuga menziesii*]. Oregon Douglas Fir. 87-feet [26.52 metres].
*Taxus baccata*. Common Yew. 50-feet x 10-feet 7-inches [12.24 x 3.23 metres].
*Thuja dolobrata* [*Thujopsis dolabrata*]. Hiba. 25-feet [7.01 metres].
*Castanea sativa*. Spanish or Sweet Chestnut. 80-feet x 13-feet 6-inches [24.38 x 4.11 metres].
*Eucalyptus globulus*. Tasmanian Blue Gum. 60-feet [18.29 metres].
*Fagus sylvatica*. Common Beech. 80-feet x 9-feet 4-inches [24.38 x 2.84 metres].
*Liriodendron tulipifera*. Tulip Tree. 68-feet x 8-feet 2-inches [ 20.73 x 2.49 metres].
*Quercus ilex*. Holm Oak. Recorded but no dimensions given.
*Quercus pedunculata* [*Q.robur*] Common Oak. 78-feet x 10-feet 4-inches [23.77 x 3.15 metres] and 70-feet x 7 feet 5-inches [21.34 x 2.26 metres].
*Quercus suber*. Cork Oak. Specimen noted as 'an old tree with spreading boughs 9-feet 7-inches girth at 1-foot up'
*Tilia vulgaris*. Common Lime. 78-feet x 11-feet 7-inches [23.77 x 3.53 metres].

# APPENDIX 3

## Trees and Shrubs in the Tollymore Pleasure Grounds in 1937

The following is a transcription of a list of the 'Trees and shrubs in the Pleasure Ground' at Tollymore compiled in August 1937 by Elinor, Countess of Roden. Some botanical names have changed since 1937, so to avoid any confusion the modern plant names, where appropriate, have been inserted in brackets after the given names; the spelling here follows the *Hillier Manual of Trees and Shrubs* (6th edition, 1991). The Latin names in the original manuscript have not been italicised.

### 'On the left of the… from small gate to kitchen garden. First Row'

Arbutus unedo
Cupressus lawsoniana erecta viridis [*Chamaecyparis lawsoniana* 'Erecta Viridis']
Cupressus lawsoniana aurea [*Chamaecyparis lawsoniana* 'Aurea']
Quercus suber
Cupressus pisifera squarrosa [*Chamaecyparis pisifera* 'Squarrosa']
Buddleia plumosa [?*Buddleja globosa*]
Berberis pratti (on rockery)
Cupressus lawsoniana albo spica [*Chamaecyparis lawsoniana* 'Albospica']
Pittosporum
Cupressus lawsoniana albo spira [*Chamaecyparis lawsoniana* 'Albospica']
Tilia (lime)

### 'Second Row. Down from lime tree by kitchen garden'

Three Syringa alba [?*Syringa x chinensis* 'alba']
Cupressus lawsoniana Stewarti [*Chamaecyparis lawsoniana* 'Stewartii']
Cupressus lawsoniana aurea Smithi [*Chamaecyparis lawsoniana* 'Smithii']
Cupressus lawsoniana pisifera aurea [*Chamaecyparis pisifera* 'Aurea']
Magnolia
Cupressus lawsoniana filifera [*Chamaecyparis lawsoniana* 'Filifera']
Taxus fastigiata aurea [*Taxus baccata* 'Fastigiata aurea']
Thuja orientalis
Cupressus lawsoniana erecta viridis [*Chamaecyparis lawsoniana* 'Erecta Viridis']
Cupressus lawsoniana pisifera
Cupressus lawsoniana erecta viridis [*Chamaecyparis lawsoniana* 'Erecta Viridis']
Cupressus lawsoniana pisifera

### 'From the lime tree by small gate. Third Row'

Group of Japanese maples [Acer palmatum]
Cupressus lawsoniana albo spira [*Chamaecyparis lawsoniana* 'Albospica']

View of the pleasure grounds from the west front of the house, looking north-west, circa 1870

Cupressus lawsoniana erecta viridis [*Chamaecyparis lawsoniana* 'Erecta Viridis']
Cotoneaster frigida [*Cotoneaster frigidus*]
Cupressus obtusa aurea [*Chamaecyparis obtusa* 'Aurea']
Pinus insignis or Monterey Pine [*Pinus radiata*]
Athrotaxis laxifolia – 'planted 1925; sown 1922 from seed from Stewarts'
Pinus stobrus nivea or Weymouth pine [*Pinus stobrus* 'Nivea']
Podocarpus chilinus – 'Planted 1925 by Elinor Roden' [*Podocarpus salignus*]
Cupressus pisifera plumosa [*Chamaecyparis pisifera* 'Plumosa']
Sequoia gigantea (Wellingtonia) [*Sequoiadendron giganteum*]
Taxus (two)
Criptomeria elgans [*Cryptomeria japonica* 'Elegans']

'Down from lime tree by garden gate. Fourth Row'

Thuya Dolobrata variegata [*Thujopsis dolabrata* 'Variegata']
Cotoneaster frigida [*Cotoneaster frigidus*]
Thuja orientalis
Cupressus lawsoniana albo spica [*Chamaecyparis lawsoniana* 'Albospica']
Araucaria imbricata [*Araucaria araucana*]

Cupressus pisifera  [*Chamaecyparis pisifera*]
Abies pectinata (Silver fir)  [*Abies alba*]
Cupressus lawsoniana albo spica  [*Chamaecyparis lawsoniana* 'Albospica']
Sequoia gigantea  [*Sequoiadendron giganteum*]
Lauristinus  [*Viburnum tinus*]
Thuja plicata
Cupressus lawsoniana erecta viridis  [*Chamaecyparis lawsoniana* 'Erecta Viridis']

### 'Fifth Row. From pernettya bush to upper path'

Cupressus lawsoniana erecta viridis  [*Chamaecyparis lawsoniana* 'Erecta Viridis']
Amelanchier canadense  [*Amelanchier canadensis*]
Cupressus obtusa aurea  [*Chamaecyparis obtusa* 'Aurea']
Araucaria imbricata  [*Araucaria araucana*]
Azalea bed
Cupressus lawsoniana Stewarti  [*Chamaecyparis lawsoniana* 'Stewartii']
Lauristinus  [*Viburnum tinus*]

### 'Sixth Row. From Upper Path, from Eucalyptus Tree'

Taxus
Thuya plicata
Cedrus atlantica
Pinus sylvestris (Scotch Fir)
Almond Trees
Abies Pinsapo glauca. Planted by Elinor Roden circa. 1925.  [*Abies pinsapo* 'Glauca']

### 'Up from fence by Amelanchier'

Quercus coccinea. Elinor Roden, circa 1926
Araucaria imbracata  [*Araucaria araucana*]
Cotoneaster frigida  [*Cotoneaster frigidus*]
Halesia carolina
Cupressus lawsoniana albo spica  [*Chamaecyparis lawsoniana* 'Albospica']

### 'Seventh Row. Down from Upper Path to Garden Fence'

Cupressus lawsoniana patula  [*Chamaecyparis lawsoniana* 'Patula']
Cupressus lawsoniana intertexta  [*Chamaecyparis lawsoniana* 'Intertexta']
Pinus strobus nivea  – sown 1922 by Elinor Roden  [*Pinus strobus* 'Nivea']

# *APPENDIX 4*

## Trees of the Tollymore Arboretum in 1964

The following is a list of the conifers and broad-leaved trees present in the arboretum at Tollymore in 1964. The list was published in the *Tollymore Forest Park* guide, published by the Forest Service (Ministry of Agriculture, Northern Ireland) in 1964.

*Abies alba* (Common or European silver fir)
*Abies amabilis* (Amabilis)
*Abies cephalonica* (Grecian fir)
*Abies concolor* (Colarado fir)
*Abies delavayi*
*Abies faxoniana*
*Abies forrestii* (Forrest's fir)
*Abies grandis* (Grand fir)
*Abies homolepis* (Nikko fir)
*Abies koreana* (Korean fir)
*Abies magnifica* (Magnificent fir)
*Abies nordmanniana* (Caucasian fir)
*Abies numidica* (Algerian fir)
*Abies pinsapo* (Spanish fir)
*Abies procera* var. *glauca* (Noble fir)
*Abies veitchii* (Silver fir)
*Abies venusta* (Santa Lucia fir)
*Agathis australis* (Kauri pine)
*Araucaria araucana* (Chile pine or monkey puzzle)
*Athrotaxis cupressoides* (Tasmanan cedar)
*Callitris tasmanica* (Oyster Bay pine)
*Cedrus atlantica* (Atlas pine)
*Cedrus atlantica* var. *glauca* (Atlas cedar)
*Cedrus brevifolia* (Cypress cedar)
*Cedrus deodara* (Deodar)
*Cedrus libana* (Cedar of Lebanon)
*Cephalataxus fortunei* (Chinese plum yew)
*Chamaecyparis lawsoniana* (Lawson cypress)
*Chamaecyparis lawsoniana* var. albo spica
*Chamaecyparis lawsoniana* var. erecta
*Chamaecyparis lawsoniana* var. lutea
*Chamaecyparis nootkatensis* (Nootka cypress or yellow cypress)
*Chamaecyparis obtusa* (Hinoki cypress)

A silver fir, one of the Seven Sisters, with dog cart, circa 1870

*Chamaecyparis obtusa* var. Crippsii (Hinoki cypress)
*Chamaecyparis obtusa* var. *gracilis* (Hinoki cypress)
*Chamaecyparis pisifera* var. *filifera* (Sawara cypress)
*Chamaecyparis pisifera* var. *plumosa aurea* (Sawara cypress)
*Chamaecyparis pisifera* var. *squarrosa* (Sawara cypress)
*Crytomeria japonica* (Japanese cedar)
*Cryptomeria japonica* var. *elegans* (Japanese cedar)

*Cunninghamia lanceolata* (Chinese fir)
*Cupressus duclouxiana*
*Cupressus lusitanica* (Mexican cypress)
*Cupressus macrocarpa* (Monterey Cypress)
*Cupressus sempervirens* (Mediterranean cypress)
*Cupressocyparis leylandii* (Hybrid cypress)
*Dacrydium franklinii* (Huon pine)
*Fitzroya cupressoides*
*Fokienia hodginsii*
*Ginkgo bilobo* (Maidenhair tree)
*Glyptostrobus pensilis* (Chinese deciduous cypress)
*Juniperus chinensis* var. *japonica* (Chinese juniper)
*Juniperus communis* (Common juniper)
*Juniperus communis* var. *hibernica* (Irish juniper)
*Juniperus pinchoti*
*Juniperus recurva* (Drooping juniper)
*Juniperus sabina* var. *tameriscifolia* (Savin)
*Juniperus wallichiana* (Black juniper)
*Keteleeria davidiana*
*Keteleeria fortunei*
*Larix decidua* (European larch)
*Larix eurolepis* (Hybrid larch)
*Larix leptolepis* (Japanese larch)
*Libocedrus decurrens* (Incense cedar)
*Microcachrys tetragona*
*Metasequoia glyptostroboides* (Shui-sa/water fir) [Dawn Redwood]
*Phyllocladus trichomanoides* (Tanekaha)
*Picea abies* (Norway spruce)
*Picea abies* var. *Clanbrassiliana* (Dwarf Norway spruce)
*Picea asperata*
*Picea glauca* (White spruce)
*Picea likiangensis*
*Picea mariana* (Black spruce)
*Picea omerika* (Serbian spruce)
*Picea orientalis* (Oriental spruce)
*Picea sitchensis* (Sitka spruce)
*Picea smithiana* (West Himalayan spruce)
*Pinus cembra* (Arolla pine)
*Pinus cembroides* var. *monophylla* (single leaved nut pine)
*Pinus contorta* (Shore pine)
*Pinus mugo* (Mountain pine)
*Pinus muricata* (Bishop pine)

*Pinus nigra* var. *calabrica* (Corsican pine)
*Pinus parviflora* (Japanese white pine)
*Pinus peuce* (Macedonian pine)
*Pinus pinaster* (Maritime pine)
*Pinus pinea* (Stone pine or umbrella pine)
*Pinus ponderosa* (Western yellow pine)
*Pinus radiata* (Monterey pine)
*Pinus strobus* (White pine or Weymouth pine)
*Pinus sylvestris* (Scots pine)
*Pinus wallichiana* (Bhutan pine)
*Podocarpus salignus*
*Pseudolarix amabilis* (Golden larch)
*Pseudotsuga glauca* (Colerado Douglas fir)
*Pseudotsuga macrocarpa* (Large-coned Douglas fir)
*Pseudotsuga taxifolia* (Douglas fir)
*Saxe gothaea conspicua* (Prince Albert's yew)
*Sciadopitys verticillata* (Japanese umbrella pine)
*Sequoia sempervirens* (Californian redwood)
*Sequoia wellingtonia* [*Sequoiadendron giganteum*] (Wellingtonia)
*Taiwania cryptomeroides* (Taiwania)
*Taxodium distichum* (Swamp cypress or deciduous cypress)
*Taxus baccata* (Common yew)
*Taxus baccata* var. *fastigiata* (Irish yew)
*Taxis baccata* var. *fastigiata aurea* (Golden Irish yew)
*Thuja occidentalis* (Eastern red cedar)
*Thuja orientalis* (Chinese *arbor-vitae*)
*Thuja plicata* (Western red cedar)
*Thuja standishii* (Japanese *arbor-vitae*)
*Thujopsis dolabrata* (Hibra *arbor-vitae*)
*Thujopsis dolabrata* var. *variegata* (Eastern hemlock)
*Tsuga heterophylla* (Western hemlock)

*Acer campestre* (Field maple)
*Acer laxiflorum*
*Acer macrophyllum* (Oregan maple)
*Acer negunda* (Box alder)
*Acer palmatum* var. *atropurpureum* (Japanese maple)
*Acer palmatum* var. dissectum (Japanese maple)
*Acer palmatum* var. *linearolobum* (Japanese maple)
*Acer platanoides* (Norway maple)
*Acer platanoides* var. *Schwedlerii* (Norway maple)
*Acer pseudoplatanus* (Sycamore)

*Acer pseudoplatanus* var. *purpureum* (Purple sycamore)
*Acer rubrum* (red maple)
*Aesculus indica* (Indian horse-chestnut)
*Amelanchier canadensis* (June or Service Berry)
*Aralia spinosa* (Devil's Walking Stick or Hercules club)
*Arbutus unedo* (Strawberry tree)
*Betula papyrifera* (Paper birch)
*Betula pubescens* (White birch)
*Betula verrucosa* (Silver birch)
*Carpinus betulus* (Hornbeam)
*Castanea sativa* (Sweet chestnut)
*Catalpa bignonioides* (Indian bean)
*Cotoneaster oxyacantha* var. *coccinea* (red hawthorn)
*Embothrium longifolium* (Fire bush)
*Eucalyptus coccifera* [Tasmanian Snow Gum]
*Eucalyptus delegatensis* (Giant gum)
*Eucalyptus gunnii* [Cider Gum]
*Eucalyptus johnstonii* [Yellow Gum]
*Eucalyptus urnigera* [Urn Gum]
*Eucalyptus viminalis* [White Gum]
*Fagus sylvatica* (Beech)
*Fraxinus excelsior* (Ash)
*Fraxinus excelsior* var. *pendula* (Weeping ash)
*Fraxinus ornus* (Flowering or manna ash)
*Ilex aquifolium* (Common holly)
*Ilex aquifolium* var. *aurea marginata* (Gold leaved Holly)
*Juglans nigra* (Black walnut)
*Laburnum anagyroides* (Common laburnum)
*Laurus nobilis* (Bay laurel)
*Liquidambar styraciflua* (Sweet gum)
*Lomatia ferruginea*
*Nothofagus antarctica* (Antarctic beech)
*Nothofagus cliffortioides* (Mountain beech)
*Nothofagus menziesii* [Silver Beech]
*Nothofagus obliqua* [Roble Beech]
*Parrotia persica* (Iron tree)
*Populus x euramericana* 'Gelrica' (Hybrid black poplar)
*Populus x euramericana* 'Serotina' (Black Italian poplar)
*Prunus avium* (Gean, wild cherry or mazzard)
*Quercus castaneaefolia* (Chestnut-leaved oak)
*Quercus cerris* (Turkey oak)
*Quercus ilex* (Holm oak)

*Quercus lucombeana* (Hybrid oak)
*Quercus pedunculata* (Oak)
*Quercus rubra* (Red oak)
*Quercus suber* (Cork oak)
*Robinia pseudacacia* (False acacia)
*Salix vitellina* var. *pendula* (Golden weeping willow)
*Sorbus aria* (Whitebeam)
*Sorbus aucupria* (Rowan or mountain ash)
*Tilia platyphyllos* (Large leaved lime)
*Tilia vulgaris* (Common lime)
*Cordyline australis* (Cabbage Tree).

Note: The many varieties of flowering shrubs in the arboretum were not included in the 1964 published listings. However, some height and girth measurements of the trees were included in the publication, these being:

*Sequoia wellingtonia* [*Sequoiadendron giganteum*]. 96-feet x 18-feet [29.26 x 5.49 metres]
Douglas fir. 94-feet x 14-feet [28.65 x 4.27 metres].
Monterey pine. 85 feet x 14 feet 4-inches [25.91 x 4.37 metres] (at 8 feet from ground).
Silver Fir. 80-feet x 10-feet 8-inches [24.38 x 3.25 metres].
Beech. 90-feet x 12-feet 7-inches [27.43 x 3.84 metres] ('measures almost 40 feet to the first branch')
Cork Oak. 32 feet [9.75m] with 'crown of over 57-feet' [17.37m] diameter
*Picea abies* var. *Clanbrassiliana*. 16-feet 8-inches [5.08 metres]. 'The circumference of its crown is 38-feet 9-inches' [11.81m]. Has 7-feet [2.13m] of 'bare stem', but 'with a healthy rounded top'.

Woodland with bluebells

# *APPENDIX 5*

## John Claudius Loudon's Description of Tollymore, 1844

Extract from J.C. Loudon (1844). *Arboretum et Fruticetum Britannicum*, vol. I, History and Geography of Trees, p.110.

'At Tollymore Park, in the county of Down, planted by the Earl of Clanbrassill, and now the seat of the Earl of Roden, there are some very fine trees. The soil and situation, the first ridge of the Mourne Mountains, appear to be particularly suited to the larch and silver fir, planted 60 years ago, which is 84ft. high; the diameter at 1ft. from the ground, 5ft. 2 in; at 10ft., 4ft.; and at 24ft., 3ft. 3in.; it is beautiful and evenly clothed with branches, the lower tiers of which are pendent to the ground and the circumference of the space which they cover is 160ft. The larch at Tollymore is in much estimation for its great tenacity, and it supplies masts of from 50ft. to 60ft. in length. As a selection from a great number, we take one tree, which at 80 years of age is 84ft. high; the diameter, at 1ft. from the ground, 2ft. 8in.; and 10ft. from the ground, 2ft. 3in.: another tree, at 60 years of age, is 66 ft. high; the diameter at 1ft. from the ground, being 3ft.; and at 10ft., 2ft. 3in. Among numerous fine specimens of shrubs introduced by the late Lord Clanbrassill, there is a Rhododendron ponticum, which, at 50 years of age, is 10ft. high, and covers with its unbroken mass of foliage, a space the circumference of which is 90ft. The larch at Tollymore is grown on the side of a steep hill facing the north, on a stiff gravelly substratum, which corresponds with the natural situation in which the larch is found in Switzerland, as stated by Decandolle in the Quarterly Journal of Agriculture, vol. V, p.403; and with the situations in the neighbourhood of Dunkeld, where the best larch is grown by the Duke of Athol, as stated in the account of these plantations in the Transactions of the Highland Society of Scotland, vol. XI, p163. to p219. Monteath, the Scottish forester, we are informed by Lord Roden, and also by another correspondent, considers the Tollymore larch to be very superior in quality to the generality of the Scotch or Welch larch. Lord Roden states that he uses it for all purposes whatever, and that for forming utensils it is found an excellent substitute for ash. The trees are generally felled at the age of 70 years. The rhododendrons are scattered through the woods; they are found fully as hardy as the common laurel, and many of them have attained a large size. There are many specimens of Abies excélsea var. Clanbrassilliàna, but none of them remarkable'.

# *APPENDIX 6*

## Henry Vernon to Robert Jocelyn, September 19th, 1783

Letter from Henry Vernon, Philadelphia, to Robert Jocelyn (later second Earl of Roden), at York Street, Dublin.

Right Hon^le Lord Viscount Jocelyn, Earl Rodens, York Street, Dublin

My Dear Jocelyn

I have just left a very sensible young Sweed Scholar to Linneaus, who is come to this Continent to make a collection of all the seeds of this country for his King; tomorrow he sets out by the way of the Virginias to Niagara, he has been so good as to promise me a collection of every kind, which I shall forward to you for Lord Clanbrassill early in November; the names given to them by Linneaus will be marked upon each packet, every possible attention shall be paid to their preservation.

Mr. Bertram and Mr Young, the only Botanists of this continent, have made a list of all the trees, shrubs, and plants that are native, with many useful remarks, and observations as to the soil that best suits the growth of each, it is wrote in French; printing it here was found too expensive, they therefore sold me their manuscript, it will be valuable in the hands of a noble man so very conversant in Botany as your uncle and as I have often heard you express your love for him I assure you it is with utmost pleasure I shall send it in the case with the seeds; they will be sent directed to your lordship at Lord Rodens in York Street, when they arrive do me the favour to present them to Lord Clanbrassill and desire him to accept the seeds and manuscript as a mark of respect from your friend.

The King's Proclamation respecting the commerce of this Continent with the West Indies, has stirred up every resentment that has been palliated, with the breasts of the body politick. I dined to-day with the President of the Congress our company was the generals Washington, Lincoln, Read, Howe and Patterson, and seventeen members of Congress, Dickinson author of the Farmers Letters and President of [?Pennsylvania] and Mr. Paine (author of Common Sense, answer to the Abbe Raynal, and letter to Lord Shelbourne) who formerly kept a school at Kensington near London. The proclamation was read, the frantic fire of many of the members went to a declaration of excluding all commerce with England, unless this Edict was dammed and burnt by the Common hangman. The members for New England declared their properties ruined by salt fish not being amongst the few articles named in this proclamation, which clearly was left out to favour Nova Scotia.

Tomorrow I am going with Mr. Penn to Lancaster Reading, Bethlem and return here in ten days. Shall stay a week and then go by Fort Pit to Niagara Detroit, Oswego, Fort Sleglar to Saratoga from thence to Albany; down Hudson's River to New York, then return here for the winter in March. I shall go the Charles Town, see all the Carolinas, then by sea proceed to Boston, go over New England up to Oswego, down the Lake and River. I tour once to Montreal and Quebec. I then mean to visit Nova Scotia and embark from Halifax to Europe, from every place I can find a conveyance you shall hear from me, it is pain to me to write in general, but to converse with you always gives me pleasure for I esteem you more than all the rest of mankind put together.

I beg you to do me the honor of presenting my respects to Lord and Lady Roden, your sisters, the Honourable George and Mr. Skeffington.

Amongst your many friends believe me there is not one that loves and esteems you more than your very affectionate and Faithful servant

Philadelphia Sept 19/83/                                           Henry Vernon

Two ladies and a dog on the main steps of Tollymore house, circa 1880

# Site Gazetteer

The gazetteer offers a brief description of features within the historic demesne. These include buildings, archaeological sites and other features worthy of particular notice. Each has been given a number which corresponds with an accompanying map of the demesne. The National Grid Reference (NGR) and the Ordnance Survey (OS) 1:2500 scale map number is given for each site. Included also is the Sites and Monuments Record number (SMR) for archaeological sites and the Historic Building (HB) number for those structures that have been listed or considered for listing by Built Heritage: The Environment and Heritage Service.

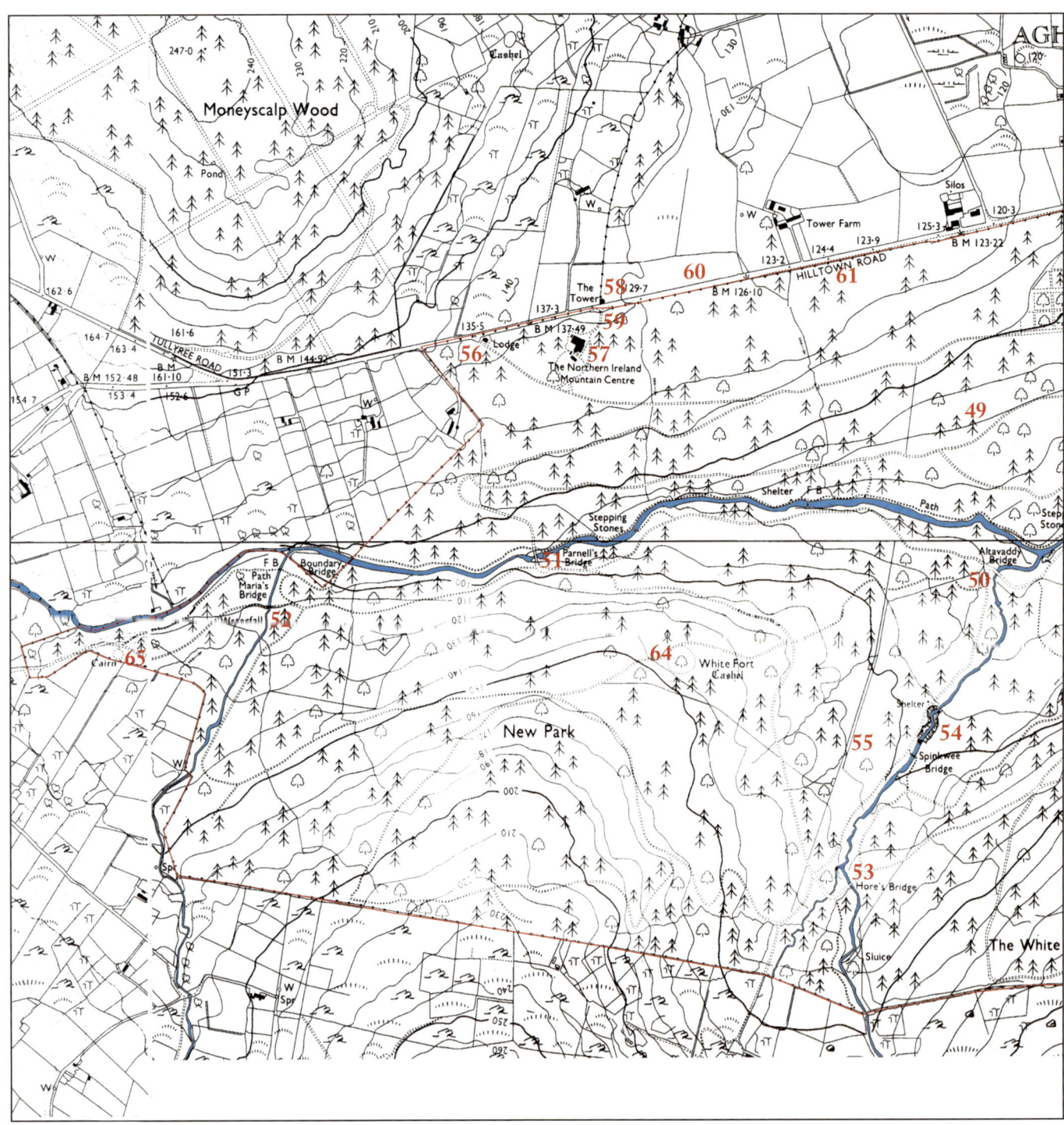

Map of Tollymore Demesne showing gazetteer sites (west section)
*Source: The 1984 edition of Ordnance Survey Sheet 255. © Crown Copyright*

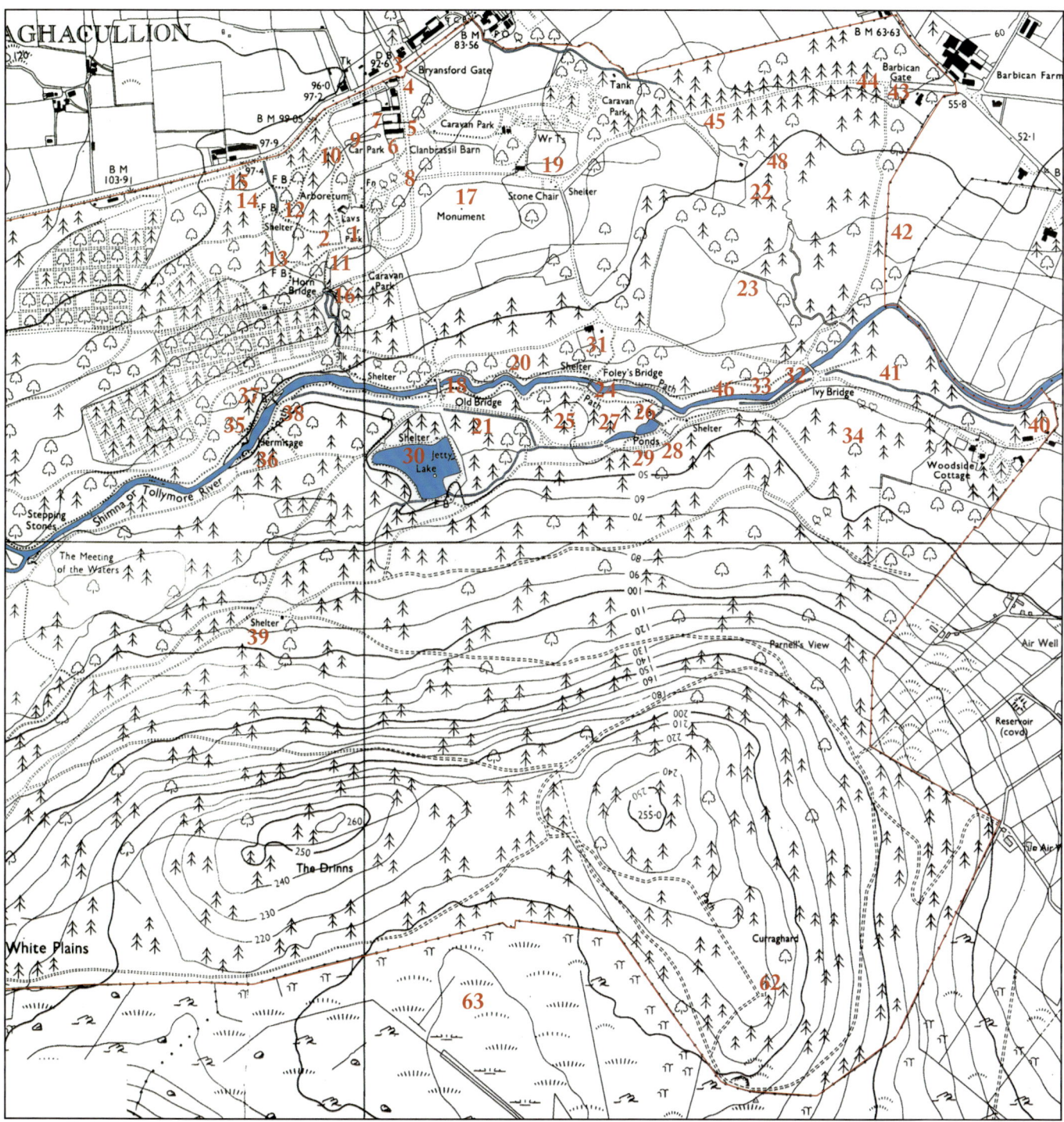

Map of Tollymore Demesne showing gazetteer sites (east section)
*Source: The 1984 edition of Ordnance Survey Sheet 255. © Crown Copyright*

The south front of the house through the trees, circa 1870

### 1. House (Site of)

Plan 255-5 SE. NGR. J343325

The family mansion, once the focal point of the demesne park, was demolished in 1952. The site, which was placed in a commanding position above the river, is now occupied by a car park. In the course of its history, the building had been remodelled and extended on several occasions. The main phases were:

Phase One: Plain south facing two storey block with one bay on either side of a central three sided bow. The bays on either side of the central canted bay had rounded-headed doorways at ground floor level. Work on this building appears to have started around 1750 for Dr Pococke, when visiting Tollymore in 1752, mentioned that Viscount Limerick had begun to build a summer residence here, described as 'a pretty lodge; two rooms of which are finished'. The house was not included on Kennedy's map of 1755, but was depicted, complete with central bay, on Scalé's map of 1760.

Phase Two: Additions to house, c.1760-77, comprising flanking one-storey three-bay wings, together with three one-storey ranges forming sides of square courtyard to the rear of the original house. The Earl of Clanbrassill, who used local craftsmen to complete the work, may have designed the additions himself. Building work must have been complete by 1777 for the

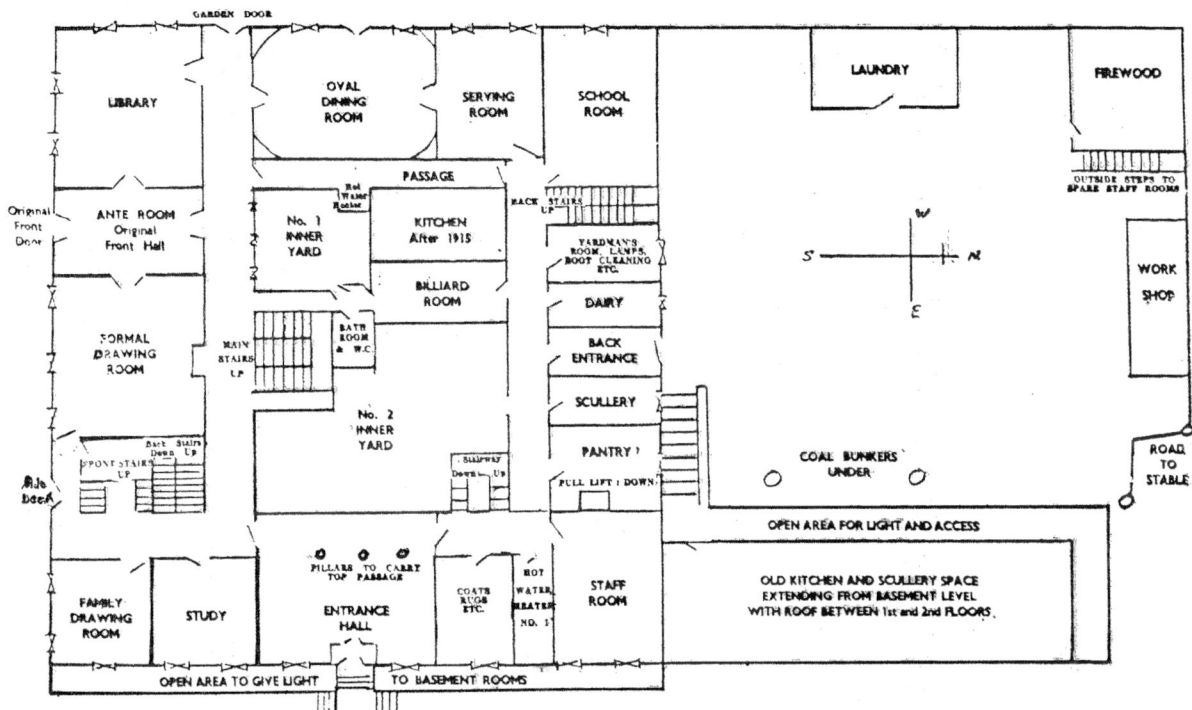

Diagrammatic sketch of the main house ground floor plan in period 1915-41

alterations were depicted on Scalé's map of that year. Ten years later the Rev. Beaufort visited the house and remarked that it had some 'very fine rooms, but too many long cold passages in the windows of which are a great many designs of painted Glass, mostly Flemish. The floors are all tiled or stucco *à l'Italienne*'. The main entrance had by that time been moved to the east range, while the west wing boasted an oval drawing room. That same year, 1787, Thomas Milton published an engraving after James Barralet., while the same building, apparently little changed, was depicted by the *Dublin Penny Journal* in the early 1830s.

Phase Three: Remodelling by third Earl of Roden, c.1838-41. The original rectangular block with its canted bay front was retained, but the flanking side wings were rebuilt as two storey ranges in a plain late Georgian style with wide eaves and granite quoins and window surrounds. The east and west ranges of the courtyard were rebuilt with nine-bay fronts, each with a three bay pedimented breakfront centre. The interior plan, with its long corridors, followed the Earl of Clanbrassill's original scheme, while the old laundry and other outbuildings in the courtyard were retained. The main house entrance remained in the east wing, but the final 1841 stage in the new improvements involved the addition of a single storey Doric portico to the entrance, complete with steps on either side of a granite ashlar perron. Also added at this time were a pair of Venetian windows set within elaborate arched recesses each side of the canted bow of the original 18th-century block. Curiously, louvred external shutters were added to all the windows on the entrance front as well as to those on the first floor of the south front; these gave the house a rather continental air.

Phase Four: The original 1750s block was accidentally burnt down in 1878, though fortunately the flanking wings were spared. Later that same year the fourth Earl of Roden commissioned

Diagrammatic sketch of the main house first floor plan in period 1915-41

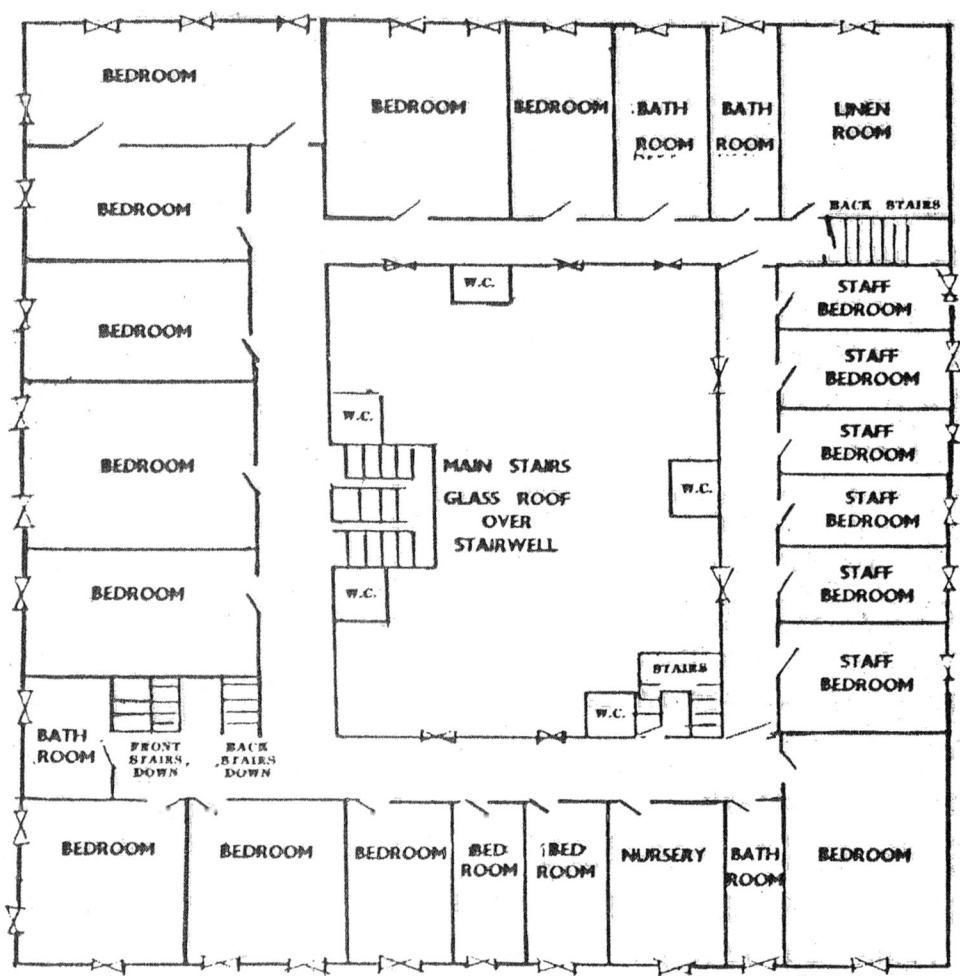

the architect James Rawson Carroll of Dublin to remodel the building. He added high mansard roofs in the French château manner to the central block, crowned by decorative ironwork and enlivened with tall chimneystacks and segmental headed dormers. Carroll also added two bands of string coursing between the ground and first floor windows on the east and south fronts and installed segmental pediments over the first floor windows of the canted bow. Also in 1878-79 all the external window shutters on the south and east front were removed.

Phase Five: In 1952 the mansion, now in the possession of the government, was demolished. The main portico was removed to Drumnaquoile, west of Seaforde, where the material was used to build an open air altar.

2. **Playing Fountain (Site)**
   Plan 255-5 SE. NGR. J3434 3256
   Base can be seen. Recently planted rhododendrons cover an area each side of it.

3. **Bryansford Gate and Front Walling** (Listed HB 18/13/019a)
   Plan 255-6 NW. NGR J34483288
   A magnificent and very distinctive granite gothic gate with flanking screens, dated 1786 and

based on a design by Thomas Wright. The central carriage entrance is through a tall but delicate pointed arch, supporting a crenellated parapet with crocketed pinnacles at the corners. There is a date stone below the parapet on the frieze '1786', while the arch spandrels just below this have unique trefoil ornaments composed of three rounded stones radiating from a central 'bap' stone. The gateway is supported by foiled flying buttresses decorated with granite balls on their outer facing. The flanking screen contains a pair of pointed arched pedestrian entrances, both with wrought iron gates with spear-head rails and concave tops, which may date to the early 19th century. The main carriage gates are more ornate and must have been installed in the late 19th century for they appear on photographs of circa 1900. However, earlier photographs of circa 1860 show that these gates were preceded by elegant scrolled ironwork gates, which presumably were original to the structure. Inside are the remains of a small porter's office with Gothic casement window. Here visitors to Tollymore would sign their names in a visitor's book. The sweep outside the gateway has a quarter circle of large 'bap' stones.

4. **Bryansford Gate Lodge** (Listed HB 18/13/019b)
   Plan 255-6 NW. NGR J34463287

   Pretty single storey gothic lodge of 1802 secreted to one side of the avenue to the west of the gates. The building was sympathetically extended at the east end some time post 1859 when a bedroom was added; less satisfactory kitchen and bathroom extensions were made to the west and rear sides in the 1970s. The front, which faces south, was originally symmetrical and comprised a centrally placed pointed arch doorway flanked by pointed arch windows; with the addition of another pointed arch window to the east end, post the OS maps edition of 1859, the building inevitably became asymmetrical. The doorway has a plain fanlight, timber sheeted door and a plain surround, incorporating a small date stone '1802'. All three of the front windows have Georgian paned sliding-sashes, while the east end has a centrally placed double lancet sash window. The walls are fine rendered, the slate roof is hipped and has two rendered chimney stacks.

5. **Clanbrassill Barn** (Listed HB 18/13/023)
   Plan 255-6 SW. NGR. J34483277

   A long rectangular building with octagonal tower and spire. The barn is depicted on Scalé's demesne map of 1777 and is labelled as 'Coach House'. The name 'Clanbrassil' would suggest a date sometime between 1756 and 1760, as the title was conferred in 1756. The 'barn', erected in the style of Wright, was probably designed by Lord Clanbrassill himself and imitates a small scale country Gothic church. Its random rubble walls have small slates and flints in the mortar joints to imitate medieval galletting practice, while window openings and doors have ashlar granite surrounds. There are granite pinnacles in each corner of the building and at the west end there is a small bellcote-like structure with a crocketed spire. The north side, which once faced into the stable yard, has a central pointed-arched pend door and random pointed-arched doors and ventilators on both floors. The south side also has a large central pointed archway with flanking rectangular windows on the ground floor and pointed-arched ventilators above. At each end there is a door with pointed-arched fanlights over a granite lintel, both being flanked with glazed windows with similar ventilators over each doorway. The large central archway on both

The Clanbrassill Barn and adjoining arch

sides gave access to a covered passage or pend, which allowed coaches through the building from the yard to the north.

The east end of the 'barn' is crowned with a short square base with three bands of granite string coursing. This supports an octagonal tower 11 feet 2 inches (3.40m) high with pointed openings on each face, some louvered, some blind. Above there is a cornice with eight slender granite pinnacles. In the centre rises a granite spire, 17 feet 10 inches (5.44m) high, which tapers up to a bap-stone, which forms the base of a weathercock. On the south face of the belfry is a sun dial with a clock above; the latter was built in 1785 by Rudhall of Gloucester. Lord Clanbrassill recorded the tower as having been 'finished in 1789'. In the 20th century the building was used as a store until the 1970s when it was converted into a lecture theatre and exhibition centre.

6. **Decorative Gateway** (Listed HB 18/13/023)
    Plan 255-6 SW. NGR. J34473276

    Adjoining the south side of the east gable end of the Clanbrassill Barn stands a delicate gothic archway, built around 1780 in the manner of Wright. This gateway provides access from the Bryansford Avenue to a small yard flanking the south side of the barn; from here the coaches could access the stable yard through the covered pend in the Clanbrassill Barn. The gateway is flanked by square piers with pointed-headed panels, surmounted by ashlar hexagonal pinnacles with pointed-headed panels on each face; each pinnacle is capped with ogee-shaped surmounts with acorn finials. The archway itself is set within what could be mistaken for an enormous crocket, whose coping is decorated with two rows of bap stones; at the apex there is a circular stone carved in a lozenge shape, surmounted by an acorn finial.

7. **Stable Yard (Site)**
    Plan 255-6 SW. NGR. J344327

    Courtyard offices flanking the east side of the walled garden. Demolished in the 1930s, the yard comprised two L-shaped ranges flanking the north side of the Clanbrassill Barn with a gap for an entrance in the centre of the north side. Carriages could also enter through the covered pend through the centre of the Clanbrassill Barn. The yard is depicted on the first OS map edition and must therefore have been built sometime between 1780 and 1834. It occupied an area that in 1777 was included in the walled garden. Robert Adam (1782-1792) provided plans for a tower at Tollymore circa 1769, incorporating a clock and a peel of bells; this was never built, but may have been part of an early scheme for this yard.

8. **Bryansford Avenue**
    Plan 255-6 SW

    Yew, evergreen oak, Spanish chestnut, cedar, and beech line the avenue. Remains of a yew avenue to left of walled garden led from back gate just to west of Bryansford gate through the Clanbrassill Barn to the rear of the house.

9. **Walled Garden (Site)**
    Plans 255 NE & 255-6 SW. NGR. J344328

    The walled garden, now largely a car park, lay to the west of the Clanbrassill Barn. It occupied an area of about five acres (2.02ha) and was subdivided into two main areas by a wall running roughly west south west on line with the tower of the Clanbrassill Barn. The garden was probably created in this form during the late 18th century; it replaced an earlier kitchen garden shown on Scalé's demesne map of 1777, which occupied the area between the Clanbrassill Barn and the Old Deer Park boundary to the north (the line of this wall remained the north boundary of the garden into the 19th century). On Scalé's demesne map of 1760 this area of the walled gardens is shown as a nursery.

The two areas of the walled garden were united by a path running down through the centre on a north-south axis. Typically, the garden contained a combination of fruit, vegetables and flowers and was designed to serve both as a functional kitchen garden and an ornamental garden. The main focus was centred upon a dramatic glasshouse, which lay in the south-west sector of the northern part of the garden (2.73 acres). This was set back from but parallel to the dividing wall of the garden and comprised two substantial lean-to ranges flanking a dramatic conservatory in the centre. Made of wood, this conservatory was essentially a long rectangular building, whose long sides supported a gabled glass roof. The deep lean-to ranges, which would have contained a vinery and probably also a peach house, had shallow pitched roofs with sliding frames to permit ventilation. The glasshouse is depicted on the 1859 OS map edition and was probably built in the 1840s.

A remarkable early photograph of the walled garden, dating to about 1865, shows that the area between the glasshouse and the dividing garden wall (itself surmounted with urns), was highly ornamental with statues and urns on pedestals interspersed with ornamental trees, light metal pergolas (probably supporting roses) and espalier fruit lining paths on metal rails. Behind this glasshouse lay a small frame yard, while against the north wall of the garden there was a long narrow lean-to range, including a melon house, demolished by the 8th Earl of Roden.

**10. Summer House (Site)**
Plan 255-5 SE. NGR. J34373271

Summer house site, marked on 1859 OS map edition on the west side of the outside wall of the walled garden.

**11. Fountain (Lion's Mouth)** (Listed HB 18/13/024)
Plan 255-5 SE. NGR. J343325

Small classical ornamental fountain, consisting of a cube-like granite block with panelled face, chamfered base and pediment. It has a boss-like decorative moulded roundel to the front face and small moulded lion's head as water outlet. Located in the Pleasure Grounds on the path just above the Horn Bridge. Uncertain date, possibly Regency, c.1810. Depicted on the 1859 OS map edition, but apparently not on the 1834 sheet (possibly an oversight).

**12. Pleasure Grounds.**
Plan 255-6. NGR.J34333242

On Scalé's demesne map of 1760 the area west of the house was marked as nurseries. While the area west of the house and north of the Horn Bridge was undoubtedly some form of pleasure ground from the 1780s, it was substantially developed from around the 1840s. This work was accompanied by the diversion of a small stream westwards and the building of a couple of summer houses. The grounds, comprising informal paths meandering between shrubs and exotic trees, was the main focus of a good tree collection.

**13. Diverted Stream**
Plan 255-5 SE. NGR. J342326

Small stream diverted westwards sometime between 1834 and 1859, presumably to accommodate creation of pleasure grounds.

The Lion's Mouth Fountain

### 14. Summer House (Site)
Plan 255-5 SE. NGR. J34133262

Site of a summer house, shown on the 1859 OS map.

### 15. Dog Kennel (Site)
Plan 255-5 SE.  NGR. J 34163268

Marked 'Dog Kennel' on Scalé's 1777 map. Still shown but not labelled on 1834 OS map edition; afterwards removed.

### 16. Horn Bridge (Listed HB 18/13/025)
Plan  255-5 NE.  NGR. 34333247

Single pointed-segmental span bridge in rubble stone, now harled, over subsidiary stream on south side of pleasure grounds. Built circa 1780 in the style of Thomas Wright, this small bridge has blind quatrefoil niches on both faces of spandrels, crennelated parapets that end in capped piers with semi-circular niches; they end in square piers surmounted by egg-shaped dressed granite domes. The recessed niche in each pier is said to have once displayed stag's horns.

**17. Monument** (Listed HB 18/13/034)

Plan 255-6 NW. NGR. J34593263

Tall granite obelisk, 25 feet high, on tapered die with pediment top and acroteria. Four inscribed slate tablets at base; the inscription (in English) on the west side reads: 'Erected by his father to the Hon. James Bligh Jocelyn R.N. who died 10th July 1812 aged 23'. He was the second son of the 2nd Earl. One of the other panels has a Latin eulogy; another has a couplet in Italian and the third has a short English verse. Located on a slight rise in park lawn and once surrounded by railings.

**18. Old Bridge** (Listed HB 18/13/030)

Plan 255-6 SW. NGR. J34543229

Single span bridge with elliptical arch over Shimna River. Built of granite and Silurian rubble, it has dressed granite (red) voussoirs and parapets with rough vertically set coping incorporating a panel 'I H 1726'. There is another on the opposite side which reads 'repaired 1822'. However, the bridge seems to have been at least in part rebuilt after 1822. The parapets are splayed at each end and the carriage over the bridge is today lined with concrete. The bridge is labelled 'Old Bridge' on 1834 map but as 'Strange's Bridge' on 1859 map. Originally the long straight avenue from Bryansford gate extended down to this bridge, as shown on Scalé's 1777 map, and it is likely this is the bridge mentioned by Walter Harris in 1744 as being 'of hewn stone'.

Two suspension bridges, one each side of the main bridge structure, are shown on late 19th-century and early 20th-century photographs. The supporting iron for these can still be seen under the bridge's arch, as well as securing points and steps.

A large boulder to the north west of the bridge is inscribed to the memory of David Stewart (1885-1970), 'the father of state forestry in N. Ireland'.

**19. Stone Chair** (Recorded HB 18/13/69)

Plan 255-6 SW. NGR J34773267

The seat is broad measuring 1.25m wide and is over 1m high with a narrow seat 0.33m wide. Inscription on back of this seat (now barely distinguishable) reads:

Here, in full light, the russet plain extend,

There, wrapped in clouds, the bluish hill ascend,

Even the wild heath displays her purple dyes

And 'midst the desert, fruitful fields arise.

**20. Inscribed Erratic**

Plan 255-6 SW. NGR. J34773232

A split glacial erratic in a cleft of rock on the north river walk between the Old Bridge and Foley's Bridge. Sometimes known as the 'River Drive Rock'. When the trees had been cleared around it, the 3rd Earl of Roden ordered stone-masons to inscribe its broken-off face with his choice of biblical instruction: 'STOP look around and praise the NAME of HIM who made it all' (John 1:3).

Date-stone on Foley's Bridge

### 21. Mill Race
Plans 255-6 SW & 255-5 SE

Mill race running just south of Old Bridge and parallel to course of river. First depicted on the 1859 OS map.

### 22. Nursery (Site)
Plan 255-6 SW. NGR. J351326

Marked as nursery on the 1834 and 1859 OS maps, and clearly the main tree nursery on demesne at this time.

### 23. Aviary (Site)
Plan 255-6 SW. NGR. J35173248

Marked and labelled 'Aviary' on 1859 map, on edge of open parkland.

### 24. Foley's Bridge (Listed HB 18/13/031)
Plan NGR. J34843229

A pretty single semi-circular span footbridge in granite and Silurian rubble over Shimna River, inscribed '1787' and 'Ht. Foley' in well crafted script. The bridge's arch, with span of 25 feet, rises 21 feet high above the river carrying a gently sloping path that curves outwards at each end. The distance from the centre of the arch to the top of the parapet is 4 feet. Each face is embellished with a series of dressed semi-circular boulders (bap stones) inset around the arch. Set in the middle of each parapet is a large undressed granite boulder; the downstream one is inscribed 'Ht. Foley' and the upstream one '1787'. The inscription probably refers to one of Lord Clanbrassill's two young nieces, both called Harriet. Lord Clanbrassill himself married Grace Foley in 1774.

### 25. Nursery (Site)

Plan 255-6 SW. NGR. J347322

Small square area of 0.94 acres, marked on OS maps (1938) to south west of Foley's Bridge. Not shown on 1859 ad 1834 editions. Tree nursery.

### 26. Old Hermitage (Site)

Plan 255-6 SW. NGR. J34953225

Marked as 'The Old Hermitage' on Scalé's 1777 map, but is not shown on the 1834 and subsequent OS map editions. This would indicate that the building was not of a very solid construction and was most likely a thatched building built of gnarled wood uprights in the style of the period. It was located south east of Foley's Bridge and on the north side of what was once a small stream that was transformed in the 19th century into a mill race with the two mill ponds; the site lay just north of the larger of these two ponds.

It is likely that the Old Hermitage was the 'thatched house' noted by Dr Pococke on his visit to Tollymore in 1752: 'just over the rivulet Lord Limerick has built a thatch'd open place to dine in, which is very Romantick, with a stove near to prepare the Entertainment'. This 'thatched house' was also mentioned by the Duchess of Leinster in 1748 as a place where 'you have dined …almost every day'.

### 27. Seven Sisters

Plan 255-6 SW. NGR. J348322

A group of seven giant silver fir trees near the Old Hermitage. Probably planted in the 1850s.

### 28. Saw Mill (Site)

Plan 255-6 SW. NGR. J34993222

Marked 'saw mill' on the 1834 and 1859 OS map editions, this was a wooden rectangular building with the date '1828' inscribed on the front gable. The building was designed to resemble a Swiss mountain chalet. Its construction was accompanied by the building of a mill race and a couple of mill ponds. Aside from the usual demesne and estate needs for home produced timber products, such as repairing buildings or making cart wheels, the mill's timber was also used for boat building and the manufacture of implements and was later exported from Tollymore for use on the Irish railways and for English coal pits.

### 29. Mill Ponds and Race

Plan 255-6 SW. NGR J322349

Two small connected mill ponds to west of saw mill and first depicted on 1859 OS map.

### 30. Mill Pond

Plan 255-6 SW. NGR. J343321

Large mill pond, 2.59 acres extent, lying directly to the south of Old Bridge. Not shown on the 1834 or the 1859 OS map editions and was probably created in the later 19th century. It was made by building a substantial dam across the stream and was intended to provide a much greater reservoir of water for the saw mill. The sluice gate lay just south of centre of the dam, letting water into a mill race that joined the 1820s mill race a short distance further east.

Date-stone on Clanbrassill (Ivy) Bridge

### 31. Dog Kennels (Jackie's Cottage)
Plan 255-6 SW. NGR. J348324

Square enclosure with buildings on north side, located just north of Foley's Bridge. Depicted on 1834, 1859 and subsequent OS editions. On Haliday's map of 1856 it is shown as a gamekeeper's cottage. The building, now known as 'Jackie's Cottage, is an early Victorian gabled single-storey cottage with a four bay front incorporating projecting sash windows under decorated barge-boards.

### 32. Clanbrassill Bridge/Ivy Bridge (Listed HB 18/13/033)
Plan 255-6 SW. NGR. J352323

A single span bridge in granite and Silurian rubble, with segmental arch and roughly dressed voussoirs, built in the manner of Thomas Wright. The parapets of fieldstone rubble with coping of flat stones incorporate a dressed panel set in the centre of the west side with the inscription '1780'; and in the opposite parapet a similar panel with letter 'C' surmounted by a coronet (monogram of the 2nd Earl Clanbrassill). At both ends the bridge's wide parapet splays outwards close to separate small square roughcast turrets with castellated surrounds and pyramidal spires in vee-jointed granite ashlar; each of these turrets has pointed niches in each face, some extending to ground level to permit use as a shelter. The bridge is marked 'Ivy Bridge' on the 1834 and subsequent OS map editions.

### 33. Suspension Bridge (site of)
Plan 255-6 SE. NGR. J353323

Site of suspension bridge, depicted in early photograph close to Clanbrassill Bridge. No trace of features associated with this structure have survived.

**34. Larch Lawn (Site)**
   Plan 255-6 SW. NGR. J 353322

   Formerly a triangular opening in woodland, shown on 1834 map and labelled 'The Larch lawn' on 1859 and subsequent editions.

**35. Hermitage** (Listed HB 18/13/035)
   Plan 255-5 SE. NGR. J34173219

   Built 1770s by Lord Clanbrassill in memory of his friend the Marquess of Monthermer, who died in 1770. It stands perched about 20 feet above a long meandering pool on the Shimna River and appears to spring naturally out of the rocks; indeed, the back wall of the structure is formed of the rock face. The outer walls are composed of mortared sharply pointed tufa style stones enclosing a main chamber 12 feet long and 8 feet wide with domed ceiling. It is entered at each end through pointed-arched openings, while two further openings face out onto the river below. The main approach is from the east via a set of stone steps and a narrow path with timber fencing. Inside the main chamber, which is a roughly circular cell with domed and corbelled roof, there is a stone slab bench against the back wall and an alcove that once contained a bust with a Greek inscription commemorating the Marquess of Monthermer. There is now a square stone panel with carved wreath. From the smaller second chamber there are steps leading up to the beech woods above. In 1823 the structure was described by Alexander Atkinson, who wrote: 'The Hermitage, which you approach by a deep descent from the lawn, is composed of a huge mass of rough stones piled up together and forming, in the interior, a chamber 12 feet by 8, with a sort of arched doorway, on each end, and two open spaces of similar form, but much larger, on the river side. In this homely hermitage (the meditations of whose inhabitant are rendered solemn by the murmuring of the river), a stone bench, the full length of the enclosure, has been arranged for his couch or resting place. The planted hill, which forms the opposite bank of the river, confines the hermit's attention to the romantic scenery of his cell, and shuts out every foreign object, every illusive scene of that lower world to which he has bid adieu'.

**36. Hermitage Suspension Bridge (Site)**
   Plan 255-5 SE. NGR. J34183218

   Former suspension bridge spanning Shimna River slightly upstream from the Hermitage. Some securing points still in place. First depicted on the 1859 OS map edition and demolished in 1936. The narrow foot bridge was supported on chains, which held iron uprights holding a planked walkway. After 1936 it was replaced with a wooden bridge just downstream (see below).

**37. Wooden Foot Bridge and Weir**
   Plan 255-5 SE. NGR. J34233226

   A wooden bridge was first erected at this point in the late 1930s to replace the suspension bridge upstream. Located close to the sluice-gate that once controlled the flow of water from the river into the saw mill race; part of the sluice gate is still present.

**38. Visitor's Dining Hall (Site)**
   Plan 255-5 SE. NGR. J34243224

   Depicted on the 1859 OS map edition as a small rectangular building placed close to the banks of the river and labelled 'Visitor's Dining Hall'. Also depicted on the 1938 map revision,

Suspension Bridge with ladies sitting below by river, circa 1870

but not shown on the first OS map edition of 1834. No trace remains and was most probably of wooden construction. This building may be one and the same as 'Pepys Cottage', which according to the Roden Papers was "fitted up for dining in".

### 39. Gamekeeper's Lodge/Huntsman's Lodge (Site)

Plan 255-9 SE. NGR. J34233185.

Depicted on maps as a rectangular enclosure with buildings on north side. Shown on Scalé's 1760 and 1777 map on subsequent OS map editions, 1834, 1859 and 1938. Labelled 'Gamekeeper's lodge' on 1859 map and 'Huntsman's lodge' on Scalé's 1777 map.

### 40. East Gate Lodge (Recorded HB 18/13/070)

Plan 255-6 SE. NGR. J35743218

A plain one-and-a-half storey gabled three bay lodge of rubble stone. It has a symmetrical north front with a projecting gabled porch in the centre bay. Above the door is a recessed trefoil or shamrock feature with datestone 'A.D.1865'. The door is flanked by small windows with timber

Barbican Gate from the west side

batten shutters with shamrock motifs. The building has dressed quoins and the ground floor windows are dressed in brick. Built on the demesne road from Ivy Bridge towards Newcastle. Used as a store by the Forest Service for many years, but in 1999 was renovated as a holiday home.

### 41. Old Mill Race
Plan 255-6 SW. NGR. J3532
Labelled 'Old Mill Race' on 1859 OS map.

### 42. Deer Park Boundary
Plan 255-6 SW & 255-5 SE
Eastern Boundary of original deer park as shown on Scalé's 1777 map.

### 43. Barbican Gate (Listed HB 18/13/037)
Plan 255-6 SW. NGR. J35433286
Gothic barbican gate at the eastern approach to the demesne. It has a pointed arch gateway flanked by round castellated towers, built around 1780. The gateway comprises a tall central

pointed arch surmounted by a castellated parapet with supporting brackets of small bap stones and quatrefoil shaped loops in the spandrels. The gates are of plain wrought iron with spear heads and curved tops. The two flanking towers have bevelled bases, a mid level string course, a blind trefoil windows in the first floor (both towers) and a castellated parapet supported by brackets of small bap stones. The ground floor of both towers contains a pointed doorway; the north side door serves as an pedestrian entrance to the demesne, while the other entrance on the south side gives access to the tower from the west. This has a timber door and leads to a spiral staircase, where it is possible to climb to the top of the tower. The 'doorway' on the opposite (east) side of this south tower is 'blind'. The gateway is not indicated on Scalé's 1777 map and was made in the wall of the original deer park, set back from road.

### 44. Barbican Gate Lodge (Site)
Plan 255-6 SW. NGR. J35423288

A rectangular gate lodge was formerly located on north side of gates. It was built circa 1810 and was a single storey three bay symmetrical lodge with castellated parapet disguising a hipped roof. Constructed of rubble stone – windows had large diagonal glazing patterns. Demolished.

### 45. Main Avenue
Plan 255-6 NW & 255-6 SW

Line of avenue inside Barbican Gate through parkland. In 1805 the area flanking this avenue was transformed into a small twenty-six hectare deer park.

### 46. Stone Chair (Recorded HB 18/13/32)
Plan 255-6 SE. NGR. J35093228

Remains of a boulder granite seat located on the north side of the river, close to the path between Clanbrassill (Ivy) Bridge and Foley's Bridge. The boulder, which is about 1 metre high, has an inscription on its south face, a coronet surmounting an 'R' and 'River Drive 1868'. The 'seat' of the 'chair' is a slightly larger granite block.

### 47. Lower Paddock
Plan 255-6 NW.

Labelled 'Lower Paddock' on Scalé's 1777 map – open parkland flanking the avenue inside Barbican Gate. Area formed part of twenty-six hectare deer park formed here in 1805.

### 48. Lime Kiln (Recorded HB 18/13/36)
Plan 255-6 SW. NGR. J35223272

Remains of a rubble-built lime kiln that is marked on Scalé's 1777 map as 'Lime House'. The kiln has been long abandoned but its hearth with segmental arched head of stone voussoirs on the east side is recognizable. No doubt this kiln was the one used to produce lime mortar for all the building work at Tollymore in the later 18th century.

### 49. Ruined Building
Plan 255-5 SE. NGR. J336322

Long rectangular stone rubble building, 9m x 4.5m, engulfed in the woods north of the Shimna River, on the edge of what was formerly open parkland. The end gable wall, which faces

The Stone Chair on the River Drive

north with a height of circa 5m, contains a pointed arch with eleven 'bap' stone set in the wall face outside the voussoirs. More such stones lie in the debris nearby. Function of structure is not established.

**50. Altavaddy Bridge** (Delisted HB 18/13/026)
Plan 255-9. NGR. J336319
Single-span rubble stone bridge with dressed voussoirs. Built sometime between 1780 and 1800. Located south of the meeting of the waters and carried drive over the Spinkwee River.

**51. Parnell's Bridge** (Delisted HB 18/13/027)
Plan 255-9. NGR.J327320
A handsome rubble stone single-span carriage bridge over the Shimna River, with datestone '1774'. It has a large single semicircular arch with dressed voussoirs and parapets with rough stone coping, splayed at the southern end. It could have been named after Sir John Parnell (1744-1801), the one time Irish Chancellor of the Exchequer and friend of the 2nd Earl, or after one of Sir John's grandsons, the Rev. George Parnell.

**52. Maria's Bridge** (Delisted HB 18/13/028)

Plan 255-9. NGR. J322319

A small handsome single-span bridge, similar to Parnell's Bridge (above). It has a semi-circular arch and low parapets with rough coping. The bridge is named after Maria Le Despenser, wife of the 3rd Earl of Roden, whom he married in 1813. It was built circa 1840.

**53. Hore's Bridge** (Delisted HB 18/13/029)

Plan 255-9. NGR. J344313

Single-span rubble bridge built over the Spinkwee River in 1824. Semi-circular arch with roughly dressed voussoirs. Low parapets with rough vertical coping. Stone inscribed '1824' in centre of one of the parapets; in centre of the other is a carved shell motif. Known for a short period as 'Nassau's Bridge', after Nassau Jocelyn, the youngest son of the 3rd Earl. The present name comes from the Rev. Walter Hore of Wexford, who married Harriet, aunt of the 3rd Earl. The initials 'W.H' are recorded as having been inscribed on one of the parapet stones.

**54. Spinkwee Cascades**

Plan 255-9. NHR. J355316

To the north of Altavaddy Bridge is a narrow cleft in the rock through which the Spinkwee River dramatically passes to a small calmer pool. In the rock there is a specially constructed viewing gallery approached down stone steps. Improvements here may be, in part, the work of Thomas Wright.

**55. Old Deer Park Boundary**

Plans 255-5 SE and 255-9 NE

East boundary of the Old Deer Park as shown on Scalé's 1777 map and still clearly present.

**56. West Gate Lodge** (Listed HB 18/13/044)

Plan 255-5 SW. NGR. J32673237

A one and a half storey rectangular Tudor-Revival lodge built 1876 to design of John Birch. This design was featured in Birch's book *Picturesque Lodges* published in 1879 and was erected much as it was illustrated. The ground floor around the building is faced with random basalt stones (granite quoins), while the first floor is finished in vertical 'black and white' half-timbering, which has been slightly jettied outwards. The three bay front, which faces south-west, is entered centrally through a dramatic gabled entrance canopied porch incorporating side benches, while the flanking windows have single cut stone surrounds; there are no first floor windows on the front elevation. The steeply pitched roof with half-hipped gable is covered in earthenware tiles completed with bonnets. The west gable end has a canted window bay at ground floor level and a projecting square window supported on decorative brackets. The east façade has a centrally placed pair of windows on both floors; between the two windows is a lozenge-shaped datestone with the inscription '1876'. There are good carved wooden gates and decorative posts surviving with this lodge.

**57. Mountain Centre** (Recorded HB 18/13/068)

Plan 255-5 SW. NGR. J32843237

A two storey log cabin-style outdoor pursuits centre built in 1970 to designs of the James

Waterfalls on the Spinkwee River, circa 1865-70

Munce Partnership for the Central Council for Physical Recreation. It has the appearance of a chalet with a roughly L-shaped plan, and trees from Tollymore were used in its construction. Located to the east of the White Gate.

### 58. Hexagonal Roadside Tower (Listed HB 18/13/043)
Plan 255-5 SW. NGR. J32883244

A hexagonal tower on a roughly circular rubble stone base lying on the north side of Bryansford-Hilltown road in Aghacullion. The sides of the tower have alternating blind gothic arches and quatrefoil loopholes. Surmounted by slender conical spirelet surrounded with three

Square Roadside Tower on the Hilltown road

diminishing rings of 'bap' stones at intervals along its length. The perimeter is enclosed with smooth oval stones set on end giving it a 'claw' like effect. The structure was originally harled and no doubt was also whitewashed. This is one of the constructions known as 'Lord Limerick's Follies' and was built circa 1780 in the manner of Thomas Wright. It is located roughly opposite the old West Entrance to demesne that is shown on Scalé's 1777 map. Marked on the 1859 and subsequent OS map editions as 'The Tower'.

**59. Porter's Lodge (Site)**
Plan 255-5 SW. NGR. J32893243

Site of 'Porter's Lodge' as depicted on Scalé's map of 1777. Former entrance to the West Avenue into Tollymore, known as the West Gate or the Hilltown Gate. The avenue had been abandoned by the time of the publication of the 1834 OS map edition, by which time the lodge had been removed. There are no records of this building and no trace survives; it may have been only a simple structure. The entrance roughly corresponds to the position of the present entrance to the Mountain Centre.

**60. Gate Pillars** (Listed HB 18/13/042)

Plan 255-SW. NGR. J33133247

A pair of cylindrical rubble rendered gateposts set in a low wall and leading into a field on north side of the Bryansford-Hilltown road. Each pier is surmounted by a conical spire with half a dozen bap stones around it. There is a loop-like slit in the south side of each pier. One of 'Lord Limerick's Follies' and built circa 1780.

**61. Square Roadside Tower** (Listed HB 18/13/040)

Plan 255-5 SE. NGR. J33363253

A tower and pyramidal spire, 2.5m square and 5.5m high. It has a square base of rubble stone, with a blocked gothic arch in front and a string course at the level of the arch impost. There is a prominent cornice, with round 'bap' stone supports at each corner, enclosing a tall stone rubble pyramid. This pyramid has 'bap' stones in each face and an ovoid acorn shaped 'bap' stone finial. Small stepped flying buttresses on each side join feature to the demesne wall. The recesses in tower represent what was once apparently a small pedestrian gateway into the demesne; on the north side this recess is now blocked with rubble. This structure is sometimes known as 'The Cut-throat Tower' (someone appears to have had their throat cut in the doorway). It is one of the constructions known as 'Lord Limerick's Follies' and was built circa 1780.

**62. Curraghard Chalet (Site)**

Plan 255-10 NW

A chalet and stables were constructed by the 3rd Earl near the summit of Curraghard (Tea House Hill) in the 1820s. Built for the more adventurous visitors to Tollymore. Not depicted on any of the OS map editions. The name Curraghard means 'marshy upland'. The area of Curraghard lying south of the Old Deer Park boundary was evidently planted on the 1780s.

**63. Cultivation Ridges (Tullybranigan)**

Plan 255-10 NW

Cultivation ridges running NE-SW over quite a large area. Appear to underlie the boundary wall of the Curraghard Plantation, indicating a date pre-1780s. The ridges are circa 2m wide (Monuments and Buildings Record, EHS, Hill Street).

**64. White Fort.** Cashel (SMR Dn 49:3; Scheduled Monument)

Plan 255-9 NW. NGR. J33053178

Large circular cashel, known as the 'White Fort', located on a south slope with ground falling to the south and west. The enclosing wall, now in a poor condition, is 3.20m thick and appears to have been made of massive blocks for the base with smaller stones for the core and upper levels. It survives to a height of 1m above the interior and 2m above the exterior. The circular interior, 44m x 54m diameter, is strewn with boulders and has been damaged in the past by cut and fallen trees, as well as machine tracks. However, there may be some surface structures within, notably

Ruined cashel walls of the White Fort, Tollymore

on the eastern edge (Monuments and Buildings Record, EHS, Hill Street). The entrance appears to have been on the south side, while a gap in the wall on the north west is probably modern. See plan on page 15.

**65. Round Cairn (The King's Grave)** (SMR Dn 49:2).

Plan 255-8 NE. NGR. J320317.

Round Cairn on the western boundary of demesne, known variously as the 'Giant's Grave' or the 'King's Grave' and located above a steep scarp over the south side of the Shimna River. The cairn takes the form of a round mound, slightly truncated to the north, with a diameter of 18m and standing to a height of approximately 2.50m (Monuments and Buildings Record, EHS, Hill Street). On top of the cairn is a circular depression 3.50m diameter, marking the 'scene of exploration about 1905' mentioned in the *Preliminary Survey of Ancient Monuments for Northern Ireland* (ed. D.A. Chart 1940, p135). The same account also noted that this excavation 'uncovered a large cist which contained a few bones and the crumbled remains of what was probably a food vessel'. This cist is not visible, but to the south east are a number of boulders which may mark a kerb. The cairn almost certainly belongs to the Early Bronze Age (2000 to 1500 BC).

# Illustration Acknowledgements

The author and publishers would like to express their thanks to all individuals, photographers, institutions, photographic agencies and publishers who have kindly supplied illustrations for publication in this book.

Ebba Kinberg Pate of Studio Minerva: pp36, 70, 76, 85, 105, 110, 181, 183, 188, 191; James McEvoy: Frontispiece, Title Page & pp7, 8, 61, 64, 67, 71, 73, 76, 78, 79, 84, 101, 112, 113, 114, 141, 165, 176, 179, 186; Gerald King: Front Cover copy of Milton original; Lane Studios, Galway: pp17, 24, 27, 34, 35, 41, 49, 50, 51, 94, 96, 102, 124, 125; © Columbia University in the City of New York, Avery Architectural & Fine Arts Library: pp56, 57, 58, 59; © The National Trust, Wallington: p60; © Sir John Soane Museum, London: p65; © The National Geographic Society, Washington DC: p109; © The Titanic Society: p108; © Trinity College Dublin, Manuscripts Department: p54; © Christie's Images, Vauxhall: p48; © Abbott and Holder, London: pp10, 19; © The Ordnance Survey, Northern Ireland: pp4, 170-1; © Ulster Folk and Transport Museum, Cultra, The Green Collection: pp9, 62, 69, 75, 77, 121; © Environment and Heritage Service, Built Heritage: pp15, 40, 193; © The Knight of Glin: p12.

Old Bridge, Tollymore, circa 1841. *Source: Hall's Ireland*